Contents

75 network marketing
experts on the...

BEST
WORST
FIRST

Everything you need to
know to build the business
of your dreams

Margie Aliprandi
Martha I. Finney

BEST WORST FIRST

Copyright © 2013 by Margie Aliprandi and Martha Finney. All rights reserved, including the right to reproduce this book, or portions thereof, in any form. No part of this text may be reproduced, transmitted, downloaded, decompiled, reverse engineered, or stored in or introduced into any information storage and retrieval system, in any form or by any means, whether electronic or mechanical without the express written permission of the author. The scanning, uploading, and distribution of this book via the Internet or via any other means without the permission of the publisher is illegal and punishable by law. Please purchase only authorized electronic editions and do not participate in or encourage electronic piracy of copyrighted materials.

The publisher does not have any control over and does not assume any responsibility for author or third-party websites or their content.

Cover art and design by Aidan Kallas

Published by Telemachus Press, LLC
http://www.telemachuspress.com

ISBN# 978-1-939927-66-8 eBook
ISBN# 978-1-939927-67-5 paperback

2014.02.18

Printed in the United States of America

10 9 8 7 6 5 4 3 2 1

DEDICATION

It's to you, of course.
To you, your dream,
and to knowing
you have
what it takes
to make it happen.
Know that you deserve it.
Know that the authentic leader in you
will benefit the lives of those
who are waiting for you right now.
Imagine:
One day you may grace the pages
of a future Best Worst First as a
Network Marketing Legend.

An Introduction from the Authors

Margie Aliprandi

You're about to go behind the scenes of network marketing through the hearts and minds of 75 experts who are shining examples of what and where all networkers want to be. They're the Real Deal. They're expressing their full potential through the most beautiful business model ever invented. They've paid the price and they're reaping the magnificent rewards. From 20-somethings to seasoned veterans with decades under their belts, they are six- and seven-figure earners who have changed lives and helped many reach similar heights. Now page after page, each one brings you the truly exquisite gifts of wisdom and practical guidance that can make a difference in your network marketing results. Anywhere, any time, for the rest of your life.

When business journalist and author Martha Finney came into my world with her unique concept for this book, I knew I must help make it a reality. I knew it could become an exceptionally rich and permanent resource of timeless inspiration and instantly actionable tips for anyone at any stage of the journey. But never did I expect such stunning results. Intimate, pithy, no-holds-barred *gems* from this diverse group of highly successful networkers, coaches, and company owners.

Martha is one of those people who, long-ago, flat-out rejected network marketing until one of those inexplicable moments when it suddenly felt so right. Long story short, we merged my 26 years of seasoned, historical perspectives with her curiosity as a newcomer. We added her exclusive Best-Worst-First interviewing technique and set out to cut to the chase with some of the most accomplished people I know.

We interviewed active network marketing experts worldwide from North America and Europe to Russia and Slovenia to China and Australia and the Philippines. They qualified by their generous openness and by the proven track records behind their abundant incomes. They are singles and couples, ages 24 to late 60s, with priceless expertise in everything from the basics to the advanced. Their business building methods range from kitchen table presentations, to social media and blogging, to going international, and everything in between.

You'll see new light being shed on familiar topics. And the re-engineering of yesterday's ways. You'll see exact strategies for how to relate, how to attract, how to lead, how to balance family and business life today. You'll see what works and what doesn't in network marketing today. And how to manage the inner game and drill down deeply into your *why*. You'll own a composite picture that answers the question: What does success in modern network marketing look, feel, and sound like right now?

As we interviewed one after another of the extraordinary leaders in this book, I heard one of my favorite themes underlying everything they said, and everything they've done – you will succeed if you persist over time.

There's a sowing season, and a reaping season, and they don't occur in the same season. Your job is to keep planting. If you plant consistently every day, the harvest will come. And when it comes you'll know you've earned it. And most likely, you'll also ask, "What did I ever do to deserve this?"

And so, I saw the heart and soul of these 75 experts. Who they really are. The gracious, magnanimous, loving character of these people who have reached the pinnacle of success validated my belief that it's who you become in the process that counts and lasts forever.

The process of network marketing requires a deeper level of personal growth than most any venture I can think of. It calls upon you to know yourself and your *why*. It compels you to challenge your fears, banish your disempowering beliefs, step out of your comfort zone, cross new frontiers of interpersonal relationships, remain strongly self-motivated, lift yourself up by your bootstraps, do the right things to attract the right teammates, help them, and lead them to do the same. Actually, life is too short to do otherwise.

MARGIE ALIPRANDI

San Diego, California
November 2013
margie@margiealiprandi.com

Martha I. Finney

As a business journalist of almost 30 years, and the author of 19 books on leadership, careers, and entrepreneurialism, I've had the honor of interviewing the CEOs of household-name companies; the CIA's top spymaster; someone who extracts scorpion venom by hand; even the founding publisher of *Rolling Stone* magazine (back when it was, like, really cool). As varied as my interviews have been throughout the years, a single theme runs like a thread throughout all my encounters:

How can people manifest their full potential of meaning, love, happiness, health, connectedness and, yes, wealth, in our modern world?

But in all these years, I never considered network marketing. Well, at least not since the secret, mysterious meeting my college roommate dragged me to in the late 70s. I remember her words exactly, "If you are my friend, you'll just come and you won't ask questions." After an evening of circles and Dixie cups of punch, we went back to our dorm room and never brought up the subject again.

So to say that, in my role as a business journalist, I consciously dismissed network marketing would be an overstatement. I just never gave it a second thought.

Fast forward to the spring of 2012. My friend Libby Gill, a former Hollywood executive and marketing expert, casually let it drop that she was exploring the network marketing model. "Whoa," I thought. Libby is the most stylish, sophisticated, business-successful person I know. If she is looking at this whole network marketing thing, maybe I should investigate the business model myself. Strictly as a business journalist, you understand.

So I began reading the profession's standards – the classics and the new books, like *The Business of the 21st Century*, by Robert Kiyosaki. And I began to get it. And then I couldn't get enough of it.

Only two questions lingered in my mind: Are there people like me in network marketing? And, what exactly do network marketers, well, do?

To find out, I decided to do what I've always done: Write a book about it. In the earliest days of my research, I met Margie. And then we decided to write this book together. That was probably one of the best days and best decisions of my life.

The people whom Margie brought into my life turned out to be a wonderful, positive, generous, smart, wise, upbeat, loving, and giving group of individuals who turned their passion for helping others into thriving businesses – where their own success depends completely on the success of the people they coach and develop. Soon, instead of asking myself, "Are there people like me in network marketing?" I found myself wondering, "How can I be more like these people?"

A word about this book's structure: Over the years of interviewing the world's best thought leaders in their respective industries, I developed the tradition of concluding my interviews with three cut-to-the-chase questions about our subject at hand:

What is the best thing you can do?

What is the worst thing you could do?

What is the first thing you should do?

Margie and I decided to use these three questions as the structure of the entire book. Margie brought all these wonderful people she has known throughout her entire career in network marketing – people who know her, trust her, and love her. And I would play the role of the "model newbie," asking all these wise, successful people the three most essential questions that would unlock their secrets to network marketing success.

I hope that as you read the following pages, you will see that, yes, people just like you are thriving in this business, and changing the lives and fortunes of millions of others.

And, yes, you can do it too.

MARTHA I. FINNEY

Santa Fe, NM
November, 2013
Martha@marthafinney.com

BEST WORST FIRST

Jordan Adler

" You need to get really good at reframing whatever crisis you're facing at the moment. Think of each new day as an Etch-a-Sketch. Turn it upside down. Shake it to get a clean slate. You can start every day fresh, and new, and excited. *"*

Best

Don't quit on a bad day.

I look at building a network marketing business the same as investing time and effort to achieve any worthwhile goal. It's the same as if you wanted to be an astronaut, a plumber, an actress, an airline pilot, a college graduate, or a mom. There is going to be a level of pain that comes with those dreams. As you grow, you're going to move through various phases of discomfort to get to the point where you're good at what you want to do. Every worthwhile effort requires this.

Network marketing is no different. But people treat it like a lottery. They try it half-heartedly and then they wonder why they didn't make any money at it.

People who are on the success track and are serious about network marketing don't experience a setback as pain. It's stretching, and it's the nature of growth.

Worst

Let crisis turn to ruin.

Companies tend to showcase people who have had great successes. As a result, it appears to new people that these people just joined a company and experienced meteoric success overnight. That sets up overblown expectations without equipping people with the understanding and skills they need to ride through crises.

They don't realize that people who have reached the top echelon of network marketing companies have experienced challenges greater than most people will experience in any other career. So they think there's something wrong with them, and they start questioning whether success in network marketing is possible for them.

Many people don't have the success that they're looking for fast enough to meet their expectations. So they quit.

First

Take action to lift your spirits.

Give yourself something to look forward to. Create the dream of your future in clear, vivid detail. And hold it in your mind so you can instantly access your vision any time you need a boost. Keep the vision that's in front of you a positive one, no matter what.

Collect success stories and listen to them regularly. Not just for the ultimate pay-off story of their success but also to learn how they weathered their challenging times. These aren't just inspirational success stories. They are instruction manuals to give you all the information and strategies you need to prevail in your own situation. Everyone who achieved success has gone through seemingly insurmountable obstacles to get to where they are. Learn from them.

Access all the resources your company already has in place to support you in your journey. Commit to listening in on all the group calls. Go to the local, regional, and national meetings, conference, and seminars. Call your upline sponsors. You're not bothering them. They *want* to hear from you. Your success is their success.

Take every and any action to be in the presence of people who have done what you want to do. Get to know their story – the challenging times as well as the happy times. Learn what they've been through to get to where they are today. When you can see that you're on the right road, even though it's bumpy at times, it will naturally lift your spirits.

Margie Aliprandi

" Nothing provides the multiplicity of gifts that network marketing does. You are challenged again and again, where you must come face to face with yourself, pull yourself up by the bootstraps, and make the choices that will keep you moving forward.

You become more expansive, more loving, more whole, more capable of contributing more meaningfully as you live a life of full expression every day. The freedom is beyond belief. Where else can you get that? "

Best

See the greatness in people.

One of the biggest things we do as leaders in our business is seeing that untapped potential in people, even before they are fully keyed into it themselves. And one of the greatest things we can do is hold that vision strong for them while they step more fully into it.

When you see and acknowledge the untapped potential in others, two very powerful things happen. First, you identify and show them the qualities they already own that will make them good network marketers. Second, they conclude that you are extremely perceptive to see what others seem to have overlooked, and that maybe you are the person they can trust with their dreams and future.

Every single person has this deep longing to be truly seen -- to be recognized as valuable and important. People are starving to be listened to as they express their hearts. Be that person who sees and hears them.

Worst

Distrust yourself.

When you first started your network marketing journey, your belief level was naturally minimal. But something stirred within you and you jumped in. There was a sense of awakening. Don't let that feeling become obscured by negative influences as you share the opportunity with people who may not understand the value of your offer.

Don't let anyone's rejection make you second-guess what you know deep down to be true. You already know going in that you will get some criticism and rejection.

Know also there will be attrition. People you have invested your heart and soul in will leave. You have to hold it all very lightly, trust the process, and continue with the "daily right business-building actions." If you do, the results you seek will come. Know what you know, what you know.

So prepare yourself in advance to prevail. Sustain your belief in your company, its products or services, and the brilliance of our business model. Most importantly, sustain your belief in yourself. And in rich, emotional detail, revisit that first spark of excitement and the clarity you experienced when you said *yes* to your opportunity.

Keep your faith in your decision vibrant. Set time aside each day to read inspiring success stories of network marketing and direct sales professionals. See yourself in those stories. The more you reinforce your true understanding through the eyes of those who have lived the dream, and have been blessed by the business model, the clearer and stronger you will be.

And finally, reinforce your belief in yourself through inner work. Remind yourself that you have everything within you that you need to succeed. Welcome this opportunity to enrich yourself from within.

First

Resolve to focus on what's right.

Remember that what you focus on expands. This includes your beliefs around your likelihood of success. Remember that all beliefs start out with a single thought. And it's repetition that transforms a single thought into a belief, regardless of its accuracy. What would you choose to repeat to yourself? I recommend, "I am a master recruiter, people listen to me, they value what I have to say, and they want what I have to offer."

Use only positive experiences and thoughts to build your belief that you are destined for success in this business. Stay focused only on what is working for you, what you did well, who said *yes,* and even who said, "I'm interested, tell me more." And remember to give yourself credit for how well you handled incidents that didn't go quite the way you hoped.

Hold top of mind the thought, "I have a gift and it's just the right thing for some people. Those are the ones I'm looking for, and they are looking for me. I am the gift-giver here." Those are the people who will be magnetically drawn to you.

Tom Alkazin

" In the beginning, our passion for network marketing was to simply solve our financial needs and desires. By the grace of God and a lot of hard work, we were able to do that. Now the passion that keeps us going is helping other people build their business. That's the thrill; that's the passion. It's the excitement of seeing all these people succeed, achieve their dreams, and have hope they never had before. "

Best

Stay passionate about your goals.

People typically begin this profession with the hope that they can do a little bit better in their lives. But the best thing they can do for themselves is take that little spark of hope and kindle it into a fire – something they can stay really passionate about for the long run.

Have realistic and worthy goals. The goals must be attainable and doable. They must require you to stretch and do something every day to improve yourself. Set achievable marks that will build your confidence.

Remember it's all about progress, not perfection. So be sure not to overwhelm yourself with grandiose objectives that are too far out to believe in realistically. You come into this business already very busy, and maybe even distracted by other aspects of your life. Just be sure to nurture goals and dreams that are within your grasp and that keep you excited about what you're doing.

It's got to be simple. It's got to be fun. And it's got to be something that you believe you can do.

Worst

Unplug from your support network.

This is a team sport. You just can't do it alone. But some people who have been very, very successful in traditional businesses have a difficult time in this profession because they discover that what they're really doing is leading a volunteer army. You can't hire; and you can't fire.

This is when a lot of people drift away. And we notice that they unplug. They're not on the calls, and they don't attend the events. Communication from them drops away. They think they can do it their way. But when you try to sing the song, "I Did It My Way," you'll never get to sing the song, "Oh Happy Day."

First

Extend meaningful invitations.

Learn how to uncover the need or desire that your prospect has. This way you can make the invitation really personal. And you can help that person understand how you can meet that need as a partnership.

Make that the reason to set up a specific appointment to get together with the person for the focused discussion. The invitation must be specific to that person and his or her needs.

Once you have identified your prospect's needs, you still have one extra step before you pick up the phone and make that call. Role play with your sponsor or with a partner whom you trust.

Conduct the practice invitation exactly how you will have the conversation when you're ready. Chances are that you won't extend the invitation face-to-face. So don't do the role-play exercise face-to-face. If you expect that you will extend the invitation on the phone, then conduct the practice invitation on the phone. That way you'll be confident and comfortable when the pressure to perform is really on.

So the first step is keeping in mind your prospect's specific needs and wants. The second step is having practiced as much as you need to well in advance of the actual call. You know what they say about the way to get to Carnegie Hall. Practice, practice, practice.

Eric Allen

" By getting caught up in the daily grind, people lose touch with their dreams. I see a bigger picture here. I can transform my life with this business model. I can create more free time. I can create more financial freedom. I can pursue dreams of mine that may have gotten lost along the way. "

Best

Show your determination to succeed.

Let people know that you're serious, that you're committed, that you're going to make this happen. And that you thought enough of them to share it with them specifically.

It's so important for people to have a strong posture when they're just beginning. They shouldn't be afraid to share their *why* with people, and actually say, "Hey! I'm excited about something! And here's why I'm excited about it!" This powerful enthusiasm will captivate people's attention and they'll want to know more about where that excitement is coming from. It's far more effective than any formal presentation can be.

Taking on a network marketing business is one of the most powerful things that people can do. To join our business, people have to make a shift in their way of thinking. They must decide that they need to make some changes now or life will never get better for them. The fear of staying the same or staying average is usually a lot stronger than the fear of getting out of their comfort zone. This is the point where they have realized that everything they want in life is just outside that comfort zone.

Worst

Take rejection personally.

The number one dream stealers are often the people you might be tempted to show the business to first –

your friends and your family. That's tough for almost everyone in the beginning because you're excited. You see a chance for you to transform your life on many levels and then boom! The people who know, trust, and like you the most are the first ones to tell you it's not going to work. Or you're crazy. Or you're going to jail. Or you're going to hell.

When I bring someone new into my business, I prepare them: "I know you're excited, and I want you to stay excited. Just don't get discouraged if not everybody sees this the way we see it. Nobody goes out and enrolls every single person they want to enroll."

First

Imagine your ideal dream team.

As soon as I enroll new people, I have them write down the 10 best people they know whom they would most want to be in business with. Not the easy 10, not their broke brother-in-law who's living at home with his parents. This is a business, not a rescue mission.

I want the top 10 – the dream team – people who know them, like them, trust them, and are positive, proactive people. These dream team members have some track record of success. It doesn't have to be with a network marketing company but they've been successful in business.

If you have a positive, vibrant person who has a great track record of success and who knows you by name, get in front of that person first.

People who have been successful in business before know that it's been their own efforts that have gotten them where they are. But if they leave their business to go on vacation for two weeks, they don't make money. Small business owners and solopreneurs can relate to that. It's lonely being in business all by yourself. But still these people know how to make business happen.

It's wonderful to see the light go on and hear that *click* when they realize, "This guy's here to help me be successful. There's an entire team behind me!"

So now you have the best of both worlds. Positive, vibrant people who have great track records already, they know how to work, and they appreciate business. And they see the added value of having that team support without losing their entrepreneurial role.

Jen Audette

" We're all so very fortunate, so blessed, and very lucky to have this opportunity. And it's so exciting to know how many lives we can each change. It doesn't matter which company you represent, the opportunity is simply amazing.

I can't believe that not every single person is in our business. My neighbor across the street is a physician. I wonder, 'Why does she want to work such long, hard hours for a salary when she could make more by continuing to bless others and having fun?' "

Best
Let belief be stronger than fear.

A lot of us enter this business convinced that we just don't have the "sales gene." And we allow that belief to hold us back. But really, it's not about selling. It's about sharing something you're passionate about. If you love a product or opportunity, why wouldn't you want to share it with people you care about? Why hold it back from them? When you love something and you talk about it, people can feel your passion, and they will at least be open to listening. They can feel your excitement.

The key to keeping your own belief alive is to remember that your mission is to serve others. For instance, right now I have a couple on my team who decided to adopt their second child. But they didn't have the necessary financial resources. I gently said to the wife, "You could do this business to simply raise the money." Just recently, she wrote on her Facebook page that she earned $600 this month, and every penny of it is going to their dream of adopting a child in Haiti. That just brought tears to my eyes.

Think of yourself as someone who offers solutions. You're not *selling* people. You're *blessing* them with your helpfulness. Who doesn't have that sales gene?

Worst
Judge people.

I have had to learn again and again not to judge people. I think judging is the worst thing that I did. I was not willing to talk to people whom I thought would never want to do anything like my business. Now I would definitely go back and talk to everybody.

Just because someone may dripping in diamonds, looks perfectly put together, and has a big, beautiful home, that doesn't mean she isn't interested in having more in her life. It doesn't mean that she wouldn't love to be with a group of women once a month and have that camaraderie and the chance to express herself. She might not have that in her life. Or take it to the other extreme: I'd see someone who looked like they may not be able to afford to do this, and think, "I can't talk to her because she would just feel bad because she doesn't have enough money to try this."

You can't judge anyone.

First

Fill your calendar.

Get in touch with everybody you know now and everyone you've known in the past. Share your *why* and tell them that you're working hard to set up appointments or parties, or whatever your business model is. Fill your days as much as you possibly can. I started my business in September and in the month of November alone I held 23 home parties. I filled my calendar, even with a full-time job. Why? Because I had a dream.

How? I asked my friends who they knew who loved to have parties. But instead of putting them on the spot, I would say, "Do you have a sister, friend, or someone you know who likes to have parties? I'm really looking to fill my calendar, so if you know of someone who'd like to help...." That's how I approached it.

A full calendar also protects your forward momentum. With a full calendar, you're always building, and there's always someone new to meet. No rejection is a final rejection, because you have another meeting or event to look forward too. A full calendar keeps you on the move and busy. So whatever happens with any given meeting, it's okay. There is someone already on your schedule who is waiting to be blessed by the solutions you have to offer.

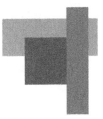

Janine Avila

" It's said, 'Build the people, and the people will build the business.' But I still get the most satisfaction watching people rebuild themselves. I've watched people get their lives back through this business. People come in broken-hearted, bankrupt, desperate, frightened. And they restore themselves to becoming who they were really meant to be.

It's such a beautiful thing. They can do it here. Be it here. Get it all back here. And I have had a front row seat on this thrill ride. **"**

Best

Take your business seriously.

You are the CEO of your business -- even if it's a part-time business. So you need to take on a CEO's mindset and behave like a CEO.

CEOs find out what they're good at and recruit people to do the other tasks. While we all believe in personal development and expanding our capabilities, CEOs delegate those tasks that they're either bad at or just plain don't want to do.

CEOs plan. Planning is a huge part of succeeding in their business. When they plan, they don't get side-tracked into ad hoc meetings or projects. They schedule their time, they identify their goals and stick to them. They take their work seriously because other people's livelihoods depend on them.

CEOs also develop others and hold them accountable. Of course, in network marketing, you have to remember that people don't want a boss, they want a leader and mentor. So learning influential and persuasive people skills is also part of taking your business seriously.

Worst

Ignore how the money is made.

Many people will just shrug and say, "I don't know how the comp plan works." That attitude may be cute for about five minutes, but it won't help you build residual income you can retire on.

If you don't take the time to understand your company's monthly business cycles, you stand to leave a lot of money on the table. All of your pay is based on that cycle. At midnight on the last day of the cycle, boom! That's the close of the cycle. The computer calculates what you get paid.

When you understand how the profit is being made, your stance goes from, "Gee, I don't know how this money shows up," to "It's a system, I've got it down." Knowing how the system works is the thing that's duplicable. Once you know it, you can take that knowledge anywhere and teach it to anyone. It's like a cake recipe. The cake will rise every time if you put certain ingredients in place.

Knowing this system behind the system alters your stance with your family and friends. You move with more confidence because you're on top of the most valuable knowledge that's part of this business. Your spouse sees that you know how to make this a money-making venture. And on that last week of the month, your friends and family know that you're focused on your comp plan and achieving your goals. During this time, you're concentrating on where you are in terms of breaking a new rank, where your team members are in terms of their own goals, who's advancing, and who needs extra attention.

First

Position yourself for success.

The late American basketball coach James "Jimmy V" Valvano said that, "To win you must first put yourself in a position to win."

Stack the odds in your favor, as much as you can. For instance, set up a physical space that you can dedicate to your business, whether you're sitting in the corner at a make-shift desk or you have a nice, separate office. Make sure it's an environment that is set up in a way that makes you feel good about what you're doing.

Set up established hours when you can dedicate your exclusive focus to your business. If you try to take care of your family, your house, your health during the exact same hours you should be concentrating on building your business, you'll risk burn-out.

Have that all-important conversation with your family. Enlist their support in your success, and help them understand that your success will benefit them as well.

Kevin & Pamela Barnum

“ **Pamela:** Financial freedom is family freedom. Our little boy gets us up every morning, not the alarm clock. We never miss a school play, anniversary, or important family events. We are in control of our schedule. So we have the freedom we want.

Kevin: In most professions, people want to bring you down rather than up. In network marketing, it's the exact opposite. As soon as people start, they see that they are surrounded by people who want to bring them along, not drag them down. ”

Best

P: Demonstrate your new success.

People may not be ready to hear about your business opportunity or product. But they will soon want to know what accounts for the changes in you. So you can just model the results and rewards you get from network marketing. You don't have to spell it out for them. People will see what's going on.

Move forward confidently. Become more professional in the way you dress or carry yourself. Take more vacations from work because you can afford unpaid time off. Look more relaxed because you're finally able to pay your bills every month, and you sleep better at night. Eventually people will want to know your secret.

K: Prepare for inevitable challenges.

In this business, you need emotional resilience. So you must set up your support systems before you need them. Our system consisted of two major parts. First was a regular schedule we committed to from the beginning. Sunday through Thursday nights we had established office hours from 8 to 10. We left Friday night open for family time. Saturdays were dedicated family days.

Secondly, we committed to ongoing learning. I started in network marketing the exact same time a coworker did. We called our morning drive into work our "rolling university." We'd listen to CD trainings on network marketing and self improvement all the way. Pam also hired a great coach to help her develop her skills.

Worst

P: Get into defensive arguments.

People teased me at work, calling me Pyramid Pam. That bothered me especially because I was a lawyer, and it was my job to know about illegal business schemes. Counteract that by taking on a leadership posture right away. You're directly diluting the stigma by presenting a professional image of a business person, rather than a desperate dog who's chasing and panting all over people to get them to try the product or business. Even if you're still the only member of your team, behave like a leader. If you take on leadership behaviors, people will come, and the success will follow.

K: Try to change people's minds.

Now we have a much simpler response when we meet people who have already formed a negative opinion about network marketing without any real knowledge. We simply ask, "What do you mean by that?" We let them explain what their objection is. And then we simply respond with, "No, that's not what it is." Then you can work on educating people from there.

First

K: Build a positive support team.

It's critical to find a few key players right out of the gate, even if they're also new. My business partner and coworker, as I mentioned, not only started the same time we did, but he also quit his job at the same time I did. It didn't matter what was going on at work, we were there to reinforce each other, strategize our business, and encourage each other to stay focused on the future and our personal development.

P: Seek out kindred spirits anywhere.

They don't even have to be in the same network marketing company you're in. Just find people who are on the same journey of personal development and growth. Look for people who have an entrepreneurial spirit and positive outlook – and who are genuine in their wish for you to be successful too. It makes a big difference in how you start.

Kody Bateman

" Network marketing is the only profession I know of that levels the playing field for all people. You can come from Yale or you can come from jail. It doesn't matter. It's not about your resume. It's not about what you accomplished in the last decade or last year. It's about what you put in today. Whatever you put into your business today, it's going to give back to you tomorrow. I love that about this profession. "

Best

Find a straight-shooting sponsor.

You want a sponsor who is going to tell you like it is. They'll tell you that it's not going to be easy, and they'll say, "If you give it a good consistent effort for two to five years, and if you follow the system that we have in place, if you can make that commitment, then we're in. I'll work with you." That's the person you want to look for in a sponsor. But most people don't look for that. That sounds too hard. They look for the over-promiser.

Find a sponsor who will expect you to take ownership of your own business, and who will take an active interest in helping you once you demonstrate that you are ready to deliver. You want a sponsor who will hold you accountable. By holding you accountable, your sponsor is role modeling how you will be holding your people accountable too.

By the same token, as a new distributor, you have to be a straight shooter, too, when you recruit prospects. You need to establish the tone of your business right away that you are serious and accountable. And that your new team members can trust that you will deliver what you promise.

Worst

Make assumptions.

Too many people assume the sales pitch provides the valid reason for joining a company, rather than relying on their common sense, good judgment, and due diligence. If you're going to be serious about starting a network marketing career, you need to know who you're in business with.

The important things to ask about a company are what is its vision and its passion and its *why*. It's far more important than how stable the company is, what kind of resume the owner has, or how much he is worth.

The biggest false assumption is that you can make big money fast: "Get in, and you can make $10,000 in your first 30 days because we're going to build it for you." A lot of people buy into that hype, and they don't make $10,000 their first month or even their first year. And then they start saying bad things about the profession.

You don't make money fast here. You just don't.

First

Find the *why* that makes you cry.

Drill down to the *whys* below the initially stated *why*. Let's say your *why* is that you want financial independence. Well, why do you want financial freedom? You say, "So I can put my kids through private school." Why do you want to do that? Continue to ask yourself why until you find that compelling answer that makes you cry.

For example, my personal *why* is to help people act on their promptings and find financial freedom. It's always been what I've wanted to do. But I had to drill down to the reason why I wanted to do that.

I lost my brother in a tragic accident, and sadly I had ignored a prompting to say goodbye to him. I never had that chance again. And I made a promise to him that I'd help myself and others act on their promptings every day.

Every time I tell that story I cry, and others do too.

That compelling *why* is what's going to keep you in network marketing. We all know it's a part-time endeavor at first. Without the compelling *why*, you dabble your feet in the water a little bit, and then you pull your feet out of the water and go do something else. That compelling *why* is going to help you stick with it.

Calvin Becerra

" Instead of sponsoring a business that looks like you, sponsor a business that looks like the world. If you could sponsor a business that looks like the world, and then let it spread globally, you'll have a business that's diversified over multiple economies. As one economy is down, another economy is up. "

Best

Sponsor "on purpose."

"Sponsoring on purpose" can mean a variety of things. If you're not a good speaker, sponsor some good speakers. If you think you're too young, sponsor some people who are older than you. If you want to enter into a particular international market, sponsor people in your own backyard who might have contacts or relatives in the countries you are targeting for eventual development.

Sponsor with the end in mind, not just for instant gratification. Build relationships early and develop a successful business locally first. Then let them take you into markets as the countries begin to open. For instance, I sponsored a friend of mine who had friends in a German networking group. As a result I was able to make friends with some of those people. Once Europe opened up, we knocked on doors in Germany and now we have a huge, established German business.

I also sponsored a Chinese-American couple in California. And they built a small business here. But once Hong Kong and Taiwan opened, their business grew there. And now because of that, we have contacts there who will eventually take us into China, which will be a huge market.

Worst

Steal prospects from fellow distributors.

This happens a lot. People decide they want to build their business in a certain location. They know that the value of their reputation as a leader will entice people to leave their sponsors and jump ship to join their teams. But when you try to build your business by destroying someone else's business, your name is ruined forever in your company.

Let's say you want to build a team in Japan, and you come into the country already equipped with a great reputation as an effective leader in other countries. People who are already in the business there see that you're coming in. And they want to leave their teams to join yours. It's tempting to bring them on, isn't it?

This is called "cross-line recruiting." Don't do it. Even if it looks to you to be a great method to build an instant team in a new location.

I have these kinds of people approach me who want to join my line, and I always turn these people away. I'm committed to building the right way. And I know people will respect me for that.

First

Build in countries that welcome you.

A market might be open in a certain country that you want to build in, but that doesn't mean that's necessarily the best choice right now. There are different cultures, and they have different attitudes toward entrepreneurs and foreigners. Some countries only want to work with their own people. Maybe there's a political or culture clash between your country and the country you'd like to begin developing.

Make sure that you have a good relationship with the management team in your target markets. If they know who you and your people are, they'll watch out for your best interests, even when you're not there. They're going to be the ones who will understand the legal and political climate. They'll be nurturing essential local relationships, supporting your teams, and developing marketing campaigns.

When you blend well with the local management team; when you're really friends with them and your hearts can mesh; that's when you create something big.

Tina Beer

" When I started this beautiful profession, I was a young woman with no college degree and no business background. But network marketing gave me the space and grace to grow and develop as a person. It gave me access to mentors I never would have been able to meet otherwise. All I had to do was put myself in a position of learning.

My life has been blessed by so many people. Now I get to be the merchant of hope for other people. "

Best

Have healthy expectations.

It's going to take three to five years to build a solid foundation that will allow for sustainable growth going forward. Don't over-estimate what you can do in a year or underestimated what's possible within five years. In the meantime, prepare yourself to welcome the trials and tribulations that you can be sure will come along the way.

They will be your greatest gift. They will shape you and be part of your compelling story. All of it is valuable. All of it matters. All of it is important. Someday it will all come together in a way that makes sense for you. And you'll be able to connect the dots. The good, the bad, the ugly. All of it is beautiful because it helps you build your business and connect with people.

Worst

Compare your journey with others'.

There's no way you can compare your life with anyone else's, no matter how parallel it may seem to yours. Unless you're walking the exact same path, in the exact same shoes, and you have the exact same fingerprints, it's a different life. And comparing your progress with someone else's story will rob you of the joy of your own journey. It brings you just unnecessary, senseless self-criticism.

Comparing yourself with others is a costly distraction. Randy Gage gave the example a couple of years ago about the importance of staying "in your lane" when you're an Olympic swimmer. One of the biggest challenges for swimmers is that they're overly concerned about what their competitors are doing in the other lanes. Randy says, "Stay in your lane, don't look left, and don't look right." Looking around actually slows you down. All you have to focus on is your performance.

Comparison can also lead to resentment. Those two things together are a deadly brew. Be grateful for all the things that happen to you – even the discouraging, disheartening things. They are your greatest gift because how you prevail will shape you. And they will form the heart of your story. All of it matters. All of it is important to you.

I understand, though, the natural urge to compare yourself with someone else. You're trying to find a gauge against which to measure your own performance and results. You're better off finding a "pace partner" – someone who will keep you inspired and accountable, and whose life is similar to yours. in terms of schedule, number of kids, background, or your career.

These are the experiences that will make you a uniquely powerful leader. No one else will have those experiences exactly the way you will. So don't look right. Don't look left. Focus on your own experience.

First

Collect success clues.

Anthony Robbins says, "Success leaves clues." So when you begin network marketing, it's your job to gather all the clues you can. Look for all the pieces of evidence that will build your growing belief in the power and credibility of this amazing profession.

Go to as many events as you can – company events, generic events, conference calls. If a meeting is four hours away, consider that a local meeting and go. It's your job to become Sherlock Holmes and gather all the clues that will build your belief in the profession and your personal success. No one can do that work for you. If you gather your own clues, you'll be able to build your own case. And then nobody will be able to break down your conviction.

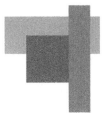

Ty Bennett

" What keeps me passionate about network marketing is the people. I love people, and I love watching them give their all, take ownership of changing their circumstances, and then succeed. This business brings out the full potential of people. And it's just the coolest thing to see! "

Best

Tell an emotionally connecting story.

At the beginning of your business you don't know all of the important facts, figures, statistics about your company. But that's okay, because ultimately people don't buy based on facts. They buy on emotion.

When you tell your story, focus on the reason you got into this business. What struggle in your life were you trying to fix? Was there a struggle with time, money, or health? Maybe you wanted to lose weight?

Every moving story is a struggle-to-solution story. So your struggle is your own personal "hook," and the solution is how you can help people. The best way to bring emotion into a conversation is to tell your story, so that you allow people to feel what you're sharing.

Worst

Try to go it alone.

I have seen so many people jump into this business thinking that they can figure it out by themselves. They don't use their upline support, three-way calling, or the expertise of the group for validation. They don't realize that they just can't succeed on a grand scale without a team behind them.

You need the team's support when you're prospecting. And your prospects need the chance to meet other people who will be on their team. Remember, you're training from the minute you start talking to a prospect. You're demonstrating the prospecting process to them, even as you're prospecting *them*. They can see first-hand how the system duplicates and how they will also be supported.

Now I've known of some very talented people who make a lot of headway early in their experience with network marketing all by themselves. But they inevitably hit the far boundary of their own limitations. They try to re-invent the wheel, and they waste time trying marketing techniques that have long ago been tried and rejected as ineffective. Or they tell a great, emotionally compelling story but mysteriously turn people off. And they can't figure out why. Or they come to the end of their warm market list and don't know how to build it back up again. Or they don't know how to get past those down days that everyone has when they feel discouraged.

That's when tapping into a team, with their resources, support, and inspiration, makes all the difference.

First

Practice your story with your mentor.

You need to tell your story smoothly and naturally. Which means you have to practice it. Practice with your sponsor. It's going to feel weird and awkward. It's going to be embarrassing. But I want you to feel comfortable with it, so that you won't botch it with the first person you talk to. The secret to sounding natural is knowing what you're going to say.

When you prepare for the role-playing experience, write down a couple of key phrases that capture the story of your struggle and why you're doing this business. Don't worry about being perfect. You can tweak it and make it better and better until you feel comfortable. And when you get to that point, that's when you're ready to call your first prospect and have that great conversation.

When you have your story down, and you're fluent in it, you can then be present and focused on the person you're talking with. You can only be extremely good at a conversation when you aren't worried about what's coming out of your mouth next – when you make it about *them*. You can focus on being interested, not interesting.

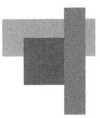

BK Boreyko

" If you knew that you could set yourself up financially for life in the next 12 to 24 months, how hard would you go at it? How much energy would you put toward it? Massive action is the key to being a success in network marketing. Be prepared to do a lot of work, but within just a little bit of time. "

Best

Have a business-like attitude.

Approach this business with the right attitude. Realize the potential of this industry and what you can create. This business can change a person's life forever. From not only a financial standpoint but also from a personal development standpoint, and a relationship standpoint.

The biggest challenge that we have is that it's too easy and too inexpensive to get started in network marketing. Ask yourself, "If I would have invested $100,000 to $500,000 to get started, how would that have impacted my attitude and approach to my business? How much better would I be at mastering the basics so that I can become great at this?" You are practicing a profession, just as if you were a doctor or an accountant.

And it's not going to be all happy high notes. You're going to have challenges. Your attitude is the one thing that you control. You decide whether you're going to have a great attitude or a bad attitude.

Worst

Need immediate gratification.

We live in a society where we stand in front of microwave and yell "hurry up!" But you have to keep in mind that you're planting seeds. You're planting seeds every time you hand over a sample or every time you engage somebody in this business. You would think that a farmer is crazy if only a month or two months after he planted his seeds, he was yelling, "Why don't I have my crop?" Your business needs time to develop the same way.

You need to give this business 12 to 24 months before you get frustrated with the results. It's much easier to go from $1,000 a month to $2,000 a month than it is to get from 0 to $1,000. It's easier because you have more invested in it.

Being relaxed about your timing and need for immediate positive results will also influence the way you approach your prospects. If you're putting pressure on yourself, you can be sure that you're pressuring your prospects to say *yes*, and say *yes* right now. Maybe some of those people will say *no* right now. But that doesn't mean that they won't sign on with you later.

You never know when the timing is going to be right for someone. A *no* right now is not a *no* forever. But if the pressure you put on yourself to be immediately successful turns you into a jerk with that person, your prospect may still say *yes* in the future, but it won't be to you.

So I think the worst thing you can do is come into any type of opportunity and expect immediate gratification.

First

Take massive action.

The biggest problem most people have is that they think they need more training before taking action. Actually they need more doing. Nothing is going to happen unless you get into action.

Don't feel like you have to be perfect before you give yourself permission to start growing your business. The key to this industry is keep everything duplicable. Don't do what doesn't duplicate.

That's the beauty of this business. When you're sitting across from someone, ask yourself, "Can this person see themselves doing this?"

You have to do what's duplicable. If it's not, don't do it.

Richard Brooke

" If it wasn't for network marketing, I'd be retiring from 40 years working in a chicken plant right about now. I would have made enough money to be buried in a lifetime of debt. I'd probably be an alcoholic, smoke two packs of cigarettes a day, and hang out in a bar.

Instead I've been to every state, province, and territory in North America at least twice, plus 20 or so foreign countries. Network marketing has gifted me with amazing personal transformation, wealth, and adventure... and still does. "

Best

Pick a company that will last.

I know this one better than most. Two out of three of mine have not. Even one that lasted 25 years is not enough...not when the 25th year approaches.

Building a successful sales organization requires at least three to five years...oftentimes more. Those are precious years you'll never get back, as well as hundreds upon hundreds of relationships you'll be exposing to the business. You'll be telling these people that this opportunity is the ultimate and that they should trust you.

But there's no such thing as residual income in a company that goes out of business. How will you know? Track record. Not promises. Not hype. Not marketing. Track record only.

Worst

Don't research company leadership.

When people first get involved in network marketing, there are usually two conditions in play. The first is that they're emotionally caught up in the excitement and possibilities of this new opportunity. They see evidence of success all around them, assume that success is within their grasp too, and then they jump in without doing their due diligence.

The other factor that drives their emotional decision is a sense of loyalty to the person who introduced them to the network marketing. When you're introduced to this business for the first time, the chances are that it's because that person is a friend, colleague, or family member. Naturally, you want to be supportive, but you need to take a serious, businesslike approach to the opportunity. You should make your company choice like you would any serious, long-term business decision.

The number one most overlooked consideration is who owns and runs the company. I would choose to join a start-up company with someone who is a die-hard, experienced network marketing leader, with the right capital reserves and the right product, much more quickly than a company that is five years old but owned by an investment bank.

You need to find the answers to these questions: Who owns the company? What is that person's pedigree in network marketing? Does he or she come from Wall Street and only see the company as an asset to sell off later? Or is this someone whose heart bleeds network marketing?

Thoroughly vet the business leaders. I'm talking financial; criminal; educational; resume; fraud; rumor; everything. I'm not looking for a Puritan. I just don't want any surprises.

First

Identify your key selection criteria.

Here are the considerations you must weigh: Will the product still be in demand in 20 years? Remember, you are working toward residual income, so the product has to be as relevant in the future as it is now. Consider the products sold by the top 20 network marketing companies. What have they been successfully selling for the last 50 to 60 years? Those are the categories of products you want to represent as well because their relevance has already stood the test of time.

Is the product something you would use even if there was no business opportunity attached to it? Is it a viable product at a reasonable price? Do you love it so much that you would be a customer in any case?

Of course you have to believe in the product yourself, but there's another reason why you have to be confident that you would use the product whether you were paid or not: Most of the sales volume is made up of distributors who quit the business but they don't quit the product. So, in a way, a main purpose for actively building an organization is to recruit the people who will ultimately be quitters. These people will always outnumber the sales leaders. And if they love the product, they will remain your customers.

Masa Cemazar

" Even though I spent 20 years in education, nothing ever gave me the opportunity to build personal development into my life like network marketing has. The chance to understand how the mind works and how to be disciplined has definitely been worthwhile. You become a richer person from the many experiences and the great people this profession brings into your life. Of course, in the meantime, you're creating a better income and a better, more healthy way to live. "

Best

Remember the younger generations.

My vision is to make network marketing a mainstream profession. By the time younger generations leave university, they should be considering network marketing as an opportunity that's perhaps equal to or even more desirable than any of the other professions.

I'm a member of the X Generation and very well educated. If I had not come across network marketing, I would be like a lot of my friends in Europe or Australia who struggle to have a well-paid job. And if they have one, they're time-poor. This is the kind of situation that makes me very determined to make network marketing a mainstream profession to give younger people a choice.

The reason I target the Y Generation is that there is a big need for leaders from this group to recruit, train, and work with their own peers.

The message for the Y Generation is very different than it is for older groups. They have different needs and interests at this point in their lives. They may not be as driven about making a lot of money or even how healthy they can be. As a group they are not likely to care about their health as much as they will be when they're 50, let's face it.

Targeting the younger generation needs to be more around entertainment. They're known for loving to do things in teams, of being part of something bigger, to be both mission- and fun-driven. This generation is moving more in groups than as individuals. They're still growing. So we focus our energies in places like universities, sports clubs, and activities groups. It's all about building life experiences with this generation. So we focus on the fun, using games, promotions, and chances to work together as teams to compete for fun prizes, like a limousine ride.

Worst

Go global before going local.

Focus on building at home until you have a stable income. Your upline can help you determine when the time is right to start expanding geographically. Then just go to the next state, and then the next. Only then should you consider going international.

From your own backyard, you can go anywhere. When you've fostered strong and deep relationships locally, those team members are also invested in expanding internationally. This creates stronger ties and a sustainable organization.

First

Meet international people locally.

Countries with diverse populations – like the United States and Australia – are perfect for this goal. You can meet people from every country in the world there. And through their contacts you can introduce your business to the people in their country.

I very much believe in building locally first and then globally. Once you have the freedom to travel, you can think about living in a foreign country for a short time and build your business exactly as you would at home. When we lived in Thailand, that's what we did. We tried to meet as many people as possible in the normal network marketing ways. We arrived in Thailand with local referrals from Australia.

Today, with so many different social media tools, you can meet people online and on the phone. But it requires a high level of skill, and it's hard to build trust. So the basic network marketing skills and techniques are your best bet when building internationally.

Onyx Coale

" Network marketing is ideally suited for women. We thrive in this business. We are already wired to create connection and community, and to make a difference in the world. This business model is where we can best leverage our natural gifts to achieve success not only for ourselves but also for our 'village.'

In network marketing, you'll find a group of people rich in love and mutual support. We care about your success and where you're going. "

Best

Be the person who attracts others.

Represent through your behaviors a quality of life that other people yearn for and resonate with. Is it healthy and happy living? A commitment to personal freedom? A calm, confident friendliness? Portray a way of life that other people want for themselves. And you will attract people who will naturally want to know more about what you're doing.

If you exude this kind of lifestyle, you will naturally have more opportunities, more friends, and more wonderful things come into your life because others hunger to be with you. It's about how you pull people in closer to you through what you stand for.

People aren't spending money like they used to. But they still have to buy the basics and take care of themselves. So, absolutely, they're in the marketplace. The difference is that they are spending money with people whom they trust and value. You need to be that person they trust and value.

Worst

Chase people.

I have a track record of signing up 90% of the people I introduced to the business. And in less than five years I was able to build an organization of 370,000 people. But just like everyone who starts in this business, I had to refine my approach. At first, I talked too much. Then I realized that the secret is in giving people time to warm up to you and the idea of network marketing.

I don't give them all the information right away. In fact, I rarely give them any information at all at first. I actually sit back and wait for people to come to me as their interest in what I'm doing increases. The most important thing is to create a depth of relationship where trust, curiosity, and a genuine connection are established first.

Even on my Facebook page, I avoid saying anything about my company. I use it to deepen relationships. When I meet new people, I ask them if they'd like to "friend" me on Facebook. It often feels much safer to people than suggesting we exchange phone numbers. This way they can watch what I'm doing, see who is in my community, and learn what I'm about. I'm giving them the chance to decide for themselves whether they'd like to be part of what we're doing. That's when they'll be open to hearing more about the business.

First

Be motivated by love of people.

I was scared to death when I first started. It wasn't natural for me to draw circles and make presentations. None of this came easily for me.

Then I made a switch in my mind and focused on simply my love of people. That comes naturally for me. So I just set the goal to meet two new people a day and decided that it was irrelevant whether they joined my network marketing business. Either way my life would be enriched, because I made a new friend and connected heart-to-heart with someone.

At that point it's not hard to introduce new friends to network marketing. The right people will see that network marketers are some of the most upbeat, positive people they'll ever meet. We spend very little time complaining; we spend most of our time talking about great friends, adventures around the world, and other life-enriching experiences. What are their other friends talking about on Facebook? The big pile of laundry in front of them and how they don't feel like doing laundry today?

It won't be long before they decide to spend their time on my Facebook page, because that's where people are talking about how much they love life.

Dana Collins

" I didn't wake up one day and decide that I wanted to sell skin care and lipstick to my friends. That's what it looks like on the surface. And as a result, many people dismiss the opportunity. But the further you get into it, the bigger it gets, the richer it gets, the more it becomes.

That's the beauty of working with people. There's a lot more love, connection, community, all those things that we crave as humans. That's one of the greatest things about this business. "

Best

Remove the option to quit.

Understand that this business that you're involved in is the vehicle that's going to give you what you want. It's going to help you realize your purpose, your *why*, and it's going to connect you with the people who will make you feel alive. I want to know what you want. Why you're doing this? Your *why* is going to connect you to your tribe. It's also how you're going to meet the people who want what you want and believe what you believe.

But if you have a back-up plan that's a fall-back position, that's where you're going to go. This is an emotional business. If you let your emotions drive the bus, it will take you to the parking lot every time.

Worst

Say: "I'll give it a try."

The worst thing you can do is say, "I'll call a couple of my friends, and if they're willing to hear about this, I'll take that as a sign that I'm supposed to do this. If they don't say *yes*, then I'm not supposed to do this." Why not just lie down in traffic? If a car hits you, then you're supposed to die today.

This is a business. You need to treat it like a business. It needs consistent effort. And you need to understand that at the beginning you're going to work really hard for very little so that later you can work very little for a lot. But if you work hard, and do it quickly, you'll have more time and money sooner.

This business is founded on basic prosperity principles. This is not a game of fate. "If it's to be it's up to me," as they say. Anyone who really wants what they want can be successful in network marketing. I know because I'm proof.

First

Be coachable.

Get out of your own way. Move your ego to the side just a little bit, recognizing that this business is counterintuitive in a lot of ways. You're going to be learning a whole new set of skills. Be coachable and just listen. Follow the leader. And do a little more than you think you should.

You don't have to reinvent the wheel. This is a very simple business. We have a tendency to make it complicated because it makes us feel like we're doing something more important. But in reality we're just making it more difficult.

This business is a transferring of belief. If I could do anything over again, I would do more sooner. The more you combine learning with doing, the more quickly you're going to find people who believe what you believe and want to join you. And the more quickly you're going to build your business and your team.

The belief comes from the doing and the reading. That will take you to the point of really enjoying the business more quickly. At one point or another we all tend to think to ourselves, "This is so simple, why do I need to read about it?" But by remaining coachable we learn how to transfer belief much more efficiently. We soon move from, "Can I do this?" to "You can do this!"

We can never stop learning how to build our belief in ourselves, our products, our business. The economy changes. Technology is constantly introducing new skills and techniques designed to make our work more efficient. But still, when you boil it all down, the brilliance of this business is the moment when we see the light in someone's eyes brighten when they get the opportunity you've presented.

To transfer that kind of belief, you must always be freshly passionate yourself. And to stay fresh like that, you are never too experienced to be coachable.

Chris Cucchiara

" This industry has transformed my life. I'm a better husband, father, a better everything because of network marketing. That's what we need to help a newcomer to the profession understand.

Yes, they're going to make money as a result of being involved in this business. But even if they didn't, who they become as a part of this business is a huge gift to themselves and their family. **"**

Best

Find a "running partner."

When you first get started in this business, you're filled with excitement, and you throw all your energy into it. But then you start to struggle, and negativity can set in very quickly. The way you counteract that is by finding what I call your "running partner" within the first three days. This person is someone you sponsor into your front line. But he or she is starting basically the same time you are, so you're really starting together, and you're learning together.

Who is an ideal running partner? Someone with the same philosophy, goals, and ambitions for the business as you have. This way you can lock arms with each other and keep each other paced with the same kind of mutual accountability. You can cheer each other on and reach out to each other when you need encouragement.

Then your running partner also sponsors a running partner, and so on. Before you know it, you have a tightly knit team of people with the same goals for your organization and a team culture of accountability. Hold "follow up Friday" meetings with this core team to review your goals for the week and to set new objectives for the following week.

If everyone sponsored a running partner, the entire network marketing profession would be twice as big as it is. It seems like such a small step, but it's a significant one. Sponsoring your first team member has to happen before anything else can. Why not make it someone you can run with; someone who shares your vision for possibilities?

Worst

Listen to negative people.

People who are new to network marketing are especially vulnerable to this. They want to share their excitement with other people – their friends and family – and the first thing that happens is that some of these friends and family members start picking the business model apart. And the new network marketers start to allow that negativity to sink into their subconscious.

Protect your new business from the dream stealers. Don't listen to them. Don't try to change their minds. Leave them alone and just bear in mind that these are the people you shouldn't be talking to right now.

When I run into negativity, I remind myself that it's not a personal attack on me. I just choose not to spend a lot of time with that person.

But that doesn't mean they don't know people who would be perfect for your business. So I've been known to say to them, "You're my friend, and I want to take care of our friendship. So I'm not asking you to join my business. But I'm looking for people just like you. Who do you know...?"

First

Know your life's purpose.

This goes beyond the surface *why*. Define what your overall life purpose is so when you do start making money, you'll know what you're going to do with that income. Your clarity of purpose will drive your dreams and goals. It's bigger than houses, cars, vacations. Those things are okay too, of course. But when you're clear on your life purpose, building this business becomes a lot more fun.

If you're driven by the deepest, most enduring *whys* of your business, you'll attract the companionship of the people who will help you get there. Your posture will be telegraphing, "I know why I'm building this business."

The way to be successful in this business is your willingness to do things that other people don't want to do. When you know what your deepest life's purpose is, you'll be more motivated to do those things, because your life's purpose is more important. And you'll be surrounded by people who care about the same things you do.

Jane Deuber

" Network marketing is the ultimate venue for personal transformation. You make relationships that enrich your life in so many different ways. I don't know of any other career I can step into where every single day I get to interact with people and make them feel special. And I am able to do this while building a beautiful business that rewards me financially. "

Best

Listen for secondary *whys.*

Most direct sellers are aware of the importance of uncovering the prospect's need, which is usually a financial need. But also look for a personal, emotional need. That way when you extend the invitation, you're helping your prospects see how their emotional needs can be met, too.

You have to be able to articulate that need back to the prospects. When you do that, you're letting them know they're being heard. In coaching, it's called, "reflecting back," which means that you repeat in your own words what you believe the prospects just said. You don't have to get it exactly right, you're just giving the prospects the chance to say, "That's kind of it, but...."

That's when their emotional needs emerge. Maybe it's a need to lead or mentor others. Or to be acknowledged for the qualities that they have. Or to have more fun in a like-minded community of positive people. Or to feel better about themselves.

When you're "reflecting back" with your prospects, you're validating that it's okay to attach emotional desires to their ambition. And you're giving them the gift of clarity about what they really need and want.

You're also holding open the possibility that the prospects may not be financially motivated anyway. I have found that the more promising prospects might already have their financial needs met. And they're looking for other meaningful ways to contribute.

By taking the time to explore their secondary *whys* but using the "reflecting back" technique, you are positioning yourself as their coach even before they sign on the dotted line. It all happens in this beautiful, safe interaction as you're mutually exploring the opportunity.

Worst

Let your inner critic run the business.

So much of the network marketing success practices are about process, scripts, and tools. But in reality, what's really driving people's success is the extent to which they let their inner critic run the show.

There are five negative emotions that everyone brings into their life: fear, doubt, worry, overwhelm, and guilt. These are the messages that the inner critic brings. When people let the inner critic run their business, they let their fear of being pushy or their self-doubt keep them from starting those essential business-building conversations.

It helps to think of your inner critic as really your protector. It's there to protect us from failure or feeling rejection. When you understand the drive behind the negative voice, it helps you hear the voice in a different way – and understand what those negative thoughts really mean.

Acknowledge the messages coming from your inner critic. Recognize that much of what you're feeling is an indication that you want to play a bigger game in your life. These negative thoughts are a sign that you're onto something big.

First

Let go of the past.

Give yourself the gift of a fresh start, even if you have a track record of falling short of success. Shore yourself up emotionally to take the new first step. Remind yourself that you are a rock star in some areas of your life, so you can take those first steps feeling really good about who you are.

Let go of any disempowering stories about yourself. "I don't follow through." "I'm not smart enough." "I don't deserve it." "I don't know enough." "I'm not good at this." These are all the stories that we wrap around ourselves.

Let them go.

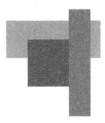

Ken Dunn

“ For the first few years of my business, it was all about making life-changing income and creating a dream life for my family. Now I have a beautiful house and big fancy cars in the driveway. But I'm too busy in the backyard having fun with my kids. That's where the joy is. And it's a euphoric feeling to meet someone new who needs what we have and who is open to discovering it.

I'm a conduit that brings this opportunity to people. This is where I want to be forever. ”

Best

Just jump in and get active.

Don't try to figure it out. Just find out how other people are achieving success in their business. And do the exact same thing. And let the momentum of their enthusiasm and positivity carry you forward.

Imagine an above-ground swimming pool packed with people standing inside the perimeter. You want to get them all moving in the same direction. At first, it's hard to move in the resistance of water. But then momentum picks up, and the water actually becomes a stream of forward moving energy. And not only is it easier to keep moving but it's actually fun. And the expression on people's faces goes from focused exertion to actual merriment.

These people have transformed themselves from a group of isolated strangers into a happy community having fun together. Who wouldn't want to join that kind of a group? Find a group just like that, with all that positive energy pushing them forward, and join in the fun.

Worst

Be a command-and-control leader.

Before I went into network marketing full time, I spent a significant amount of time as an investigative police officer. In order to do that kind of work effectively, you have to take the stance of, "Do it my way or go to jail." It took me too many years to realize that that leadership style doesn't work in network marketing. And I lost some valuable team members along the way who predictably couldn't stand working with me.

So many people enter network marketing with a work history full of leadership models that won't transfer well to this business. Instead of a strong, domineering leadership style – whether it was your own or someone you learned it from in your past – in network marketing the influential style is the most effective. You are working with volunteers in your group. They are looking to you for leadership, role modeling, and encouragement. If they feel put down or threatened in any way, there is nothing that will keep them from quitting your organization.

If you are intentionally leaving your past behaviors where they belong (in the past), choose your new role models carefully. My own first mentor was a dictator. He ruled with an iron fist. He meant well; he wanted everyone to be successful. But his methodology was terrible.

I wanted so much to be successful in this new business that I decided to do exactly what he was doing. I adopted his mannerisms, only to conclude within six months that he was a tyrant. But by that time, people were already calling me a junior version of that guy.

Find the role model whom everyone loves. Who is the person whom everyone adores and you never hear anything negative about? Model yourself after that person.

Just make sure that this person is also one of the top leaders in your comp plan. If you emulate an amazing, great person who has not achieved any significant level in the comp plan, then you've decided to model yourself after a very nice, broke person. What will that make you as a result? A very nice, broke person.

First

Commit to lifelong learning.

If you're starting network marketing for the first time in your life, you're are at the ground floor again. It doesn't matter if you were the valedictorian of your class or the CEO of your previous company. You are learning a whole new industry, and a whole new set of skills to be successful in it.

It's said that network marketing is a personal development program disguised as a business opportunity. If you take that truth to heart, and begin your career with the mindset of a newbie eager to learn, you will quickly absorb the skills and pieces of wisdom you need to start on the right foot.

And one of those bits of wisdom is embracing the great news that your new way of learning will be a way of life -- for the rest of your life.

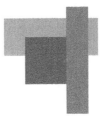

Sandy Elsberg

" Network marketing for me is an answer to prayer. It is a very luminous, exquisite opportunity for an average person to make an above-average income. It's the light at the end of the tunnel. It can soothe and quiet the pain, angst, and frustration of life for those who are stuck in a JOB, which I call the "Journey Of The Broke." It's a never-ending stream of tender mercy and grace. "

Best

Have a plan.

View building your network marketing business just as you would a decision to go to college and obtain your degree. Make the commitment from the start that you will complete your MBA. Only in network marketing, your MBA stands for Massive Bank Account, and instead of taking six years to complete, you can build a financial wall around yourself and your family in four years or less.

The big difference between going to college and building a network marketing business is that you get to earn while you learn. And, at the end of four years, you won't be looking for a job, you'll have already developed a sustainable income stream to take you where you wish to go in life.

Working directly with your sponsor is going to be a major key to your success, and your sponsor's responsibility is to help you achieve a successful start within your first 90 days. It's during this time that you will learn all the tricks and technologies of the trade and develop your motivation, management, and marketing skills necessary to build a long-term business.

Dividing up your four-year business development program into 16 separate 90-day segments will instill in you, and your new recruits, a simple, straightforward plan for working the business. Remember, your job is to duplicate the efforts of your sponsor, and then to educate and motivate your people to do the same!

Worst

Start slow.

The worst thing you can do is to let time go by without action and productivity in your first 30, 60, and 90 days. This is the period of time where you want to be focused on every activity and follow-up strategy you learn from your sponsor so that you can equate time and energy to dollars and profits.

"Don't tell me, show me," should be on the lips of every person you bring into your business. In network marketing, people will do what you do, not what you tell them to do. Individuals want to see the proof of how you got to where you are, and understand exactly how you built your monthly revenue stream into what it is today by learning your specific steps to success.

If you're not taking each day and transforming it into a positive outcome for people, product, and profit, you're losing your opportunity to demonstrate how powerful your new business opportunity is for others. This activity will give you the fast-start results you require and which you can then hold up as an example to your organization while each new person builds their 30-, 60- and 90-day story.

First

Create your story.

Just like the old adage says, "You only have one chance to make a first impression," you only have one opportunity to build your first all-important story.

If you're joining a product company, then you must 'become a product of the product,' using the product yourself, and developing your personal testimonial regarding the product benefits and what it did for you and your family. If you're joining a service company, then you must sign up for those services and develop your benefits list of how that service enriched your life and that of your family.

Once you've become a product of the product (or service), your personal testimonial will become an integral part of your recruiting and sales presentations, leading others into your particular company's path and laying the groundwork for your personal earnings story. Allowing others to see how easy it was for you to get involved, and utilize the products or services, paves the way for an exciting conversation about the business opportunity and the financial freedom that you and your business offer others.

Sean Escobar

" People don't want to be sold. They don't want to be convinced. They want to be amazed. They want to be inspired. I'm not trying to convince the world of anything. I'm looking for those individuals who are a fit. I'm qualifying people, I'm not recruiting people. What we're really selling is knowledge, inspiration, and awareness. "

Best

Focus on building teams.

I wanted to be a top income earner from the very beginning. So I focused my energy on becoming one of the top recruiters. I was signing up three or four people a day. I was just feeding the pipeline. But I found that over time I was losing everybody.

I started noticing that all the people who were winning recruiting contests weren't the big income earners. And I realized that the top income earners aren't focusing on recruiting five people a day. They know how to create community and culture and team spirit. And they know how to nurture relationships. That's what they duplicate.

When you sponsor someone, you own their success. You have to take your obligation to them seriously. So if you invest your energies and passion in building great teams with the people you have already recruited, that's when you'll start seeing the income grow.

Worst

Reject your upline's help.

When I started, I was only in my early 20s. I had to learn to be humble. I couldn't get anyone to take me seriously. That's the reality of it. I was so proud, so arrogant. I wanted to be the hero and have all the limelight. But that attitude didn't fly when I was trying to build my teams with older people. What 50- or 60-year-old wants to learn from a pup? Sure, like they're really going to say to a kid, "Teach me how to make money," I don't think so.

My parents said, "You're young, and you're going to have a hard time getting people to take you seriously. But if you can generate their interest to the extent that you can get them connected to *us*, we'll teach them the business."

So that's how I was able to succeed at such a young age. We call it "leveraging your higher authority for validation purposes." I became an expert at connecting people with the experts they would listen to and respect. I learned to say, "You ought to hear about the results my mom and dad are having with this product and the financial opportunity. I'm not the guy to talk to about this. Let me get you connected with them."

My upline told me, "Take this life experience and this wisdom and leverage it for your benefit." No matter how old (or young) you are, you'd be a fool not to take your upline up on that. But, I know first-hand, it's hard to get many young people to humble themselves and accept that support from their upline leaders.

First

Be prepared to grow – a lot.

Network marketing is personal development disguised as a business opportunity. The more you grow as an individual through personal development, self inventory, and new behavioral skill sets, the more your income will grow.

First you learn, and then you earn. It's never the other way around. I had to learn to be extremely patient. And extremely persistent. And tenacious. And disciplined.

I'm a completely different person than I was when I started eight years ago. I'm less judgmental, more forgiving, far more tolerant. I can work with so many different kinds of people, learn to adapt and adjust to their styles, use their strengths to their advantage and tolerate their weaknesses.

The better person you become, the better the people you're going to start attracting into your life. There will be a high caliber of individuals who will enter your business – provided you become one yourself.

Tony & Randi Escobar

" In network marketing, we light fires in peoples' hearts every day. There are so many people out there whose lights have gone out, and we're relighting them. That's what sustains our excitement for this business.

No matter where you come from, no matter what your history may be, or where you are in life, you can experience incredible growth in your business, your health, your wealth, and who you become as a person. "

Best

Make people feel special.

Notice people for who they are, the light that is within them, and for their specific attributes that will make them shine in network marketing. It will take extra time to connect with them on a deep, authentic level. But that approach will give them an experience that they may rarely have – the experience of being acknowledged and appreciated for their specific gifts and potential.

When you do that, you have their attention. And you've given them the gift of being able to see themselves in ways that they might have never considered before. Take the time to notice people, acknowledge that special, great personality that each one has. And then start a conversation based on even the smallest detail that is special about each person you meet.

For instance, we once met a wonderful waitress at a local restaurant. You could tell by the way she treated her customers that she loved people. We commented on that detail, which opened a special conversation with her.

We acknowledged her for her charming personality, her ability to meet and make friends with a wide variety of interesting people, and her natural enthusiasm for her work.

When the time was right, we said, "We would give anything to have you in our business." After she invested a few days thinking about network marketing, she signed on and she's doing very, very well today.

Her journey to her abundance started when she felt noticed and acknowledged for the gifts she brought to her work. And she heard the words she never expected to hear: "We would give anything to have you in our business."

Worst

Worry about the future.

Worrying never improves anything. It's an abuse of your imagination, vision, and time. It destroys your capacity for dreaming. People who fret about their future spend little time actually preparing for it.

Now is the time to reprogram your thinking and open yourself up to the potential of owning your own business. Look at your future in a different way.

Dare to be different. Dare to be bold. Every change you make now will present you with many wonderful opportunities that will enhance your life and redirect your future.

Break free from old habits and thinking patterns. Navigate a new course in your life. It's easier to do than you might think it is.

First

Prepare for the inevitable pitfalls.

Network marketing is a business of overcoming rejection, obstacles, disappointments, and discouragements. It's a business of learning from those experiences. New distributors jump into the business with an overload of enthusiasm without being prepared for coping with the negative experiences. They need to learn to reject rejection.

Knowing what the pitfalls are ahead of time – and how to deal with them – will protect you from the ultimate hazard, which is distraction. When you start to lose faith, enthusiasm, and motivation, you'll also lose focus and let distraction sidetrack you from your commitment to building your business.

It is only through absolute faith and commitment to your purpose, team work, and hard work that you will be able to avoid distractions and program your mind to succeed.

Kimmy Everett

" I want other people to experience what I've experienced. I love to see that spark in someone's eye when they understand the opportunity as I share it with them. That's the moment when their life changes. And they don't even know the greatness of what's in store for them yet.

I want to show other people this joy. We only have one shot at life, and every minute is precious. Don't waste your time doing things that don't bring you joy and value. "

Best

Take massive action right away.

The first 48 hours of your business is essential in getting off on the right foot. Plug into that system. Start your training. Set a date in your calendar when you're going to launch your business so that you have a call to action to move you forward in your first two-week period.

This is a three- to five-year commitment. And if you wait six months after you enroll to really get focused, your five-year plan starts six months in. When people hear my story, they hear, "Get rich quick." I'm an average person and I was able to create extraordinary things in a short time. And I believe anyone can do it. If they take massive action right away.

You can take massive action even if you're a single parent with a full-time job, like I was. It's about being systematic. When I first began, I did it during my lunch hour, meeting with someone new every day. And that really paid off for me. Soon, I did meetings on weekends, which I said I'd never do when I first started. Of course, that's how you build your business. Now I love meetings. It's so funny how my mindset was then and how it is now.

Worst

Take unsolicited advice.

You're going to hear everything. And the feedback you get can be crazy. That's why it's so important to have a strong *why* that drives you. Stick to your beliefs and you won't get shaken by someone else.

Don't look left. Don't look right. Just get going and keep your eye on the prize.

While I don't want you to take unsolicited advice that will discourage you, I want you to be proactive about seeking the advice that will help you build your business. With all due respect paid to your sponsor and immediate upline, also get in touch with the top earner of your company – even if that person isn't in your line.

When I contacted my company's top performer, I said, "Teach me everything you can. I'm willing to be coached, I'm willing to be told what to do, I want what you have." He could tell by the little bit of activity that I did that I would be worth his time. And so he started mentoring me. But actually he was inspiring me before we even met. I heard him on a call tell the group what he was making. It was at that point I realized that anything is possible.

First

Learn to embrace change.

Change is a part of our lives, whether we want to deal with it or not. In network marketing, there are many changes that we may not necessarily be prepared for. So if we learn to welcome change, it will be so much easier than if we resist it.

Your own life will be changing as you grow in this business. You'll discover new personal powers, new passions, new friends, and new leadership abilities that you may not have known you possessed. But at the same time, the industry will be transforming, and even your company will undergo changes.

New products may be introduced, with new formulations that you'll need to learn about. CEOs come and go. Maybe your company will merge with another, or even be sold outright. Maybe your favorite corporate staffer will find a new job and move on. Maybe your mentor leaves and it falls to you to take a new, more powerful leadership role in your organization.

Change is life. Change is growth. Something is always going to be in flux. It won't always be comfortable or even welcome. But give yourself the chance to move through your fears. You'll discover that, in a few weeks or months, that scary change is far better for you and your business than you could have ever dreamed it would be.

Todd Falcone

" There are high performers right in our own backyard who are ready and eager to hear your message. Most people don't even realize that these professional people are right underneath their nose every day. They never even initiate a phone call because they don't see the opportunity there. "

Best

Target successful professionals.

The ideal candidates are already in sales in some way. They have the drive for upward mobility, and they're already experienced in a commission-based or incentive-based environment. They would include real estate agents, mortgage brokers, sales managers, management consultants, directors of marketing, or anyone who needs to tap into their personal drive to achieve their job requirements.

Going after people like this puts the odds in your favor that you will be putting your business in front of good people who are likely to understand the quality of your opportunity. These are businesspeople who know the value of being self-employed.

For most of us, the fear of potentially failing and having to work for someone else forces us to work like no one else will. They already know what self-employment feels like. And they're typically hungry for more opportunities to build financial freedom. They get it.

Worst

Assume they won't be interested.

Entrepreneurs are really sharp people. They know the value of a great business plan that offers long-term passive income potential. As business owners (if they've been in business for very long), they understand that they must work hard for every dollar that comes in through the door. If they don't work, they don't eat. So a plan offering passive income is going to be especially attractive to the smartest of the bunch.

True entrepreneurs are already well positioned emotionally and philosophically to be receptive to hearing about other business opportunities that will provide an additional revenue stream.

First

Start noticing them all around you.

The key to being able to spot these people is to keep your eyes open and train yourself to identify them specifically. If they're in business for themselves already, they're doing everything they can to make themselves visible to potential clients. They're not hiding. They're actually marketing themselves to *you*. You just need to get in the habit of noticing them.

Be aware. Have your radar up for these people all the time. When there's a For Sale sign in front of a house, pull over and write down the realtor's name. When you're at the supermarket, do the shopping carts have placards in them advertising local services run by entrepreneurs? Notice and write down their names.

What about your neighborhood bulletin boards? Do you see any business cards tacked there that you can make note of? There's the corkboard in the coffee shop. If your community has a webpage, it might offer advertising as well. Learn to look at those ads as a wealth of possibilities for your business.

So again, who are these people? There's the mortgage broker. The real estate agent. The owner of the local cleaning franchise. The personal trainer. The management consultant. The local virtual assistant. The freelance bookkeeper. The boutique owner. Or the coffee shop owner. The caterers. Just about anyone you would meet at your local chamber of commerce mixer.

When you meet them, collect their business cards. And get ready to build your team with people who know better than anyone else how valuable it is to be independent of the typical job market, to work for themselves, and to make the real money that's out there for anyone with the nerve to be independent.

Ann Feinstein

" The sustaining passion for me is giving other people hope and watching them evolve as they allow themselves to dream again. You see magic come alive in them when they see a clear track to getting what they've been looking for.

There's nothing that excites me more than seeing the hope in people's eyes reignite. Transformation happens when people reclaim their hope. "

Best

Realize how you can help others.

The secret to living is giving. And the cumulative effect of being involved in network marketing gives you such a variety of ways to give to the world and serve something larger than yourself. Today, most companies have recognized that their success is going to be based on giving back to the communities they serve – even the ones they don't have a business presence in. So they established programs where they support local projects that benefit the total community.

My company has a foundation that gives us all an avenue to help children with serious medical needs. For instance, there was a big need for an eye clinic in Mexico. If some of the children there didn't get a certain operation by age 5, they'd be permanently blind. Imagine how desperate parents must be to know that they have to take care of this need inside a certain time frame or there will be permanent damage.

We shared the need with our entire company at convention. Within 30 minutes, we raised enough money to help 300 children.

Worst

Assume you can't make a difference.

Even if your company doesn't have a corporate foundation, there is still so much you can do on a team level. Even if you're the newest member of the team, if your team doesn't have a cause or focus already started, you can be the one to start it. Pick a focus that excites you, and recruit five, six, eight members of your team to join you in a special event. Paint a school. Do a fund-raising drive for your animal shelter. Spend an afternoon at one of the senior homes in your area. Do a clothing collection after a natural disaster, like Hurricane Sandy.

These are great team-building experiences, by the way. Building a business can be lonely – even in a social business like network marketing. This gives your local team members the chance to get to know each other in a project that is soul-fulfilling, rather just than business-oriented.

And don't overlook the public relations aspect of such an event. Take pictures of the event, and post them on your website. Even better, invite your friends to participate in the day, even if they might not be interested in the business at the moment. This is a great way for them to meet nice people who also just happen to be network marketers! Huh! Network marketers don't have horns, after all.

First

Focus on what you care about.

Don't feel as though you have to take care of every cause that comes your way. You can write a check for a cause you believe in. But when you find a cause that really tugs at your heart and soul, you will want to invest your time and energy in it. When you leverage the power of your expanded community of friends and colleagues that comes with network marketing, it's going to have much greater meaning.

It's okay to be selective on the causes you want to be personally involved with. When you're focused on those defined causes, you can attract team members who are also particularly passionate in those efforts. And you'll be spending your precious time with people who care about the same things you do.

Richard Fenton
Andrea Waltz

" **Richard:** Our enduring passion for our work comes from working with people who live their lives in pursuit of growth – and being those kinds of people ourselves. By focusing on growth, all the other things you think you want will come to you naturally.

Andrea: So many people tell us that fear of rejections has stopped them and that it's too late to change. But one small change can turn everything around. "

Best

A: Go for *no.*

Go out and intentionally increase your failure rate. Make it your goal to hear as many nos as you possibly can as fast as you can.

That's going to give you a tremendous amount of experience so you can actually learn from those nos, recraft your presentations, and gain lots of wisdom. You discover first-hand that you can survive the word no. You increase your opportunities to hear yes when you're not afraid of no.

R: Receive *yes* and *no* the same way.

One is not good and the other bad. They are simply opposites of each other -- just a reflection of someone else's preferences about what they want in their life. It has nothing to do with our value as people, or even how well we did in our presentation.

We need to stop saying, "Let's celebrate!" when we hear yes, and "Oh I'm so terrible," when we hear the word no. When we remove the emotional charges from these words we can move forward in our businesses more quickly.

Worst

R: Make decisions for others.

How many times have you thought to yourself, "Oh, that person won't be interested or receptive to what I have to say," and you use that assumption as the excu to share your opportunity with that person? What you're doing is making their decision for them, without even giving them the chance to hear you out. You're avoiding the possibility of hearing the word no from your prospect by saying no to yourself first.

Granted, rejection is bad enough for most of us when we hear no from others. Until we've neutralized yes and no, rejection is disspiriting. But when we don't even give the other person the chance to say no (or yes), that's self-rejection -- the worst rejection of all. Yes we do it all the time.

A: Let your fear of *no* paralyze you.

Learn to appreciate the fact that every time you hear the word no, it's a sign that you're in activity. If you're not in activity, you're not growing your business. So, while it might not feel like it, even hearing an unbroken string of nos is a sign that you're growing your business. You're actively getting all those rookie nos behind you, positioning yourself for hearing yes more frequently.

First

A: Use *nos* to track your progress.

Whenever we start a new venture, we want to see positive results right away. That's only human nature. But you'll experience more rejection in the beginning of building your business than any other time. So rack up those nos as a tool to keep yourself in activity, moving through a long string of them as quickly as possible. You're building your confidence and learning the processes and systems of your new business as you go.

R: Remember that *no* isn't forever.

When you're first starting your business and you hear all this rejection, you're going to be tempted to conclude that you're wasting time. But this is actually time well spent.

Many of those nos are actually seeds that will sprout later. People who say no to you now may say yes to you later when they see that you're committed to the business over the long-term and they notice how you will have grown as a person. So look at those initial nos as just the beginning of a conversation that will transform over time.

Janine Finney
Lory Muirhead

Janine: One of the most important factors to achieving success in network marketing is having unshakeable belief in what you're doing. When your belief is solid, that's when people will want to follow you.

Lory: Network marketing makes room for personal growth and the discovery of other life's passions. When I started I didn't have kids. Now that I'm a mom, network marketing has given me the chance to be financially successful while being a dedicated mom at the same time.

Best

J: Be intentional with the business.

If your goal is to see financial success, you have to be business-minded. If you treat this like a business, you'll be paid like it's a business. If you treat it like a hobby, you'll be paid like it's a hobby.

Ask yourself this question, "If my network marketing business were a job, would I still be employed, based on the effort I'm putting into my business?"

L: Commit, no matter what.

Commitment to the business was my single most useful tool when I started network marketing.

When I first started, the pain of going back to corporate America was greater than the pleasure of the possibilities. It didn't matter who joined me; who didn't join me; who thought I was crazy; who was laughing at me. Honestly, my ego didn't matter. I had no reservations. I believed it was the best decision for me.

Worst

L: Ask for your friends' opinions.

Don't give your power to other people. If you're asking for other people's opinions because you're genuinely eager for them to check out the opportunity, awesome. But if you're giving them the power to tell you whether you should continue to be doing this, that's a big red flag.

Who else lives your life? Who pays your bills? Who decides your lifestyle? No one else but you.

Remember that the people offering their opinion may not even have the life that you'd want. If the person giving you their advice and opinion doesn't have the life that you want, why would you listen to them?

J: Firehose everyone with information.

People just want to run away from network marketers who are full of pushy excitement, jargon, and tons of information about their company. Despite what many people think, growing your business is not just about you going out and getting more people. It's about coming from a place of caring about the other person.

We need to be *interested* instead of *interesting*. Be genuine and find a way to talk about this in a normal way.

First

J: Connect through your story.

Many people confuse the invitation with the presentation. Connect with people, first, and then invite them to a separate meeting to hear your presentation. Share a compelling story that they can relate to.

Talk about the things that are working in your life, and the things that you'd like to be different, and then show them how this business can be a solution. You want them to be intrigued and wanting to know more – rather than wanting to get away from you.

L: Create the "right moment."

Don't wait until you randomly happen to see people you want to share this with in the park or during a playdate. Get on the phone and create that moment with intention.

Be clear, not casual. Start out with a fact about something that's true for them. This is especially important with friends. Then say, "I believe I have found something that might be the answer for you, and I want to ask if you will sit down with me and let me just walk you through it. If you're not interested, no worries at all. I just keep thinking about you."

Doug Firebaugh

" People are looking for someone to follow in life. They want someone to believe in and someone to believe in them. Decision gives you that magnetic pull. The power of your decision radiates in your voice, gleams in your eyes, and shines in the way you communicate. People just come alive when they commit to this business and join this amazing adventure that we're all on. "

Best

Make a decision.

The reason most people don't succeed in this profession is because they're not decision-driven. They're hope-driven. Don't get me wrong. Hope is great. It's what drives people to this business. But decision precedes any successful venture, no matter what it is.

Decision changes everything. It shifts your perspective. It shifts your thinking. It shifts your expectations. And it shifts the signals that you send to your prospects. When you make a decision, you draw a line in the sand, and say, "*This* is what it is, there's no other possible option." With decision, your success becomes something that cannot and will not be denied. Make the decision that your success is something that's destined to happen.

Remember, 80% of recruitment is non-verbal. You communicate differently after you've made the decision to join this profession. People will get the message that you're serious. And they will feel your commitment on a deep emotional level That's where your power lies.

Worst

Hold expectations that are too high.

This business is so compelled by the power of vision that newcomers to the business often expect that vision to happen next week. Vision is imperative for any leader, but the challenge is that most people bring the wrong type of skills sets and thought processes into the business. They have to learn. Most people have an employee mindset. They've got to shift that.

You have to set expectations that will motivate the individual. Remember that in the first 30 days your new team members need to be active in baby steps so they can get their feet wet, understand the culture, understand all that the company has to offer, and get to know you as a leader as well. But what happens is that we do this huge vision in the beginning to get the people excited. And they expect it all to happen too soon. That takes so many people out of the profession because they conclude it doesn't work. It just didn't work on their expected calendar.

That's one of the reasons why I've routinely asked for two-year commitments. I tell them, "The odds are good that in 24 months you may not have to work anymore, but I have to know that you're at least in it for 24 months." This way your new recruits won't have unrealistic expectations, get demotivated by how long it takes, and leave the business just when things are about to break in their favor.

First

Go to your top three friends.

Sit them down and say, "I need your help as a friend." In my company, we have a Rule of 72. In 72 hours, new enrollees have to see ink strike paper. It doesn't matter whether it's an application to enroll their first prospect or it's a check for a product. To hit that Rule of 72, one of the three friends will either buy from you or sign on as a new distributor. The other two will probably lead you to someone. Or they will help you plan your grand opening reception.

Don't worry that your friends will turn you down. Bring your sponsor along to do the talking for you. Let your sponsor say, "Look, we just need your help. We're trying to get her (or his) business started. All we're doing is asking you to either refer someone, try the product to possibly purchase it, or maybe you know someone that this might be right for." Let your sponsor do the talking. You introduce them and just watch.

You don't have to go it alone.

Tyler Ford

" You're not always going to be 100% driven in your network marketing business on a sustained basis. There will always be ebbs and flows. For my wife, Mimi, and me, our passion is helping people discover a better way to fitness and nutrition.

We're motivated by more than monetary rewards. We're driven by our commitment to the war on obesity and to lead by example. The financial rewards come as a result of our dedication to the mission. *"*

Best

Set realistic expectations.

When you recruit new people, set initial goals that will require them to stretch a little bit but not overwhelm them. One of the joys of network marketing is that this business reminds and teaches us to dream big dreams. But when new people begin in the business, if the dream is too big, they get overwhelmed. They quit – and they quit fast – when their initial goals don't get met. Those pie-in-the-sky goals just set people up for frustration and failure.

This is when it's most important to set realistic expectations up front. Let them experience early success. Then you can open them up to higher and higher expectations.

Set that first goal a little lower than what you know is possible for new team members. Then when they hit that expectation, you're much more likely to keep them in your business for the long haul.

As you become seasoned as a sponsor, you learn to keep your emotions in check around setting your sites high. You keep your expectations at a level that excites and inspires you. But if you don't hit them, you know it's not the end of the world.

Worst

Don't do your due diligence.

Many people enter and then leave network marketing because they discover that they're not in alignment with the philosophy of their leadership or their company. These are things you can discover in advance of enrolling. This isn't to say that you won't find one or two people in your group you won't get along with, that's life. But it's important that overall you like your organization and what it stands for.

It's about more than simply not liking your sponsor or upline. When people discover that their leader is someone they don't want to be associated with, they shut down. They are no longer motivated to grow their business or earn a check for their upline. But they're stuck because they also have an obligation to all the people they brought in.

In the recruiting process, choose your sponsor carefully. So don't make a decision on the spot, even though you feel pressure to do so. Take the time you need to choose a sponsor who's right for you. Do you like the company? If you love the company, but you don't like the culture of the team that you've been introduced to, consider the possibility that you might gel with another team. Yes, someone's feelings might be hurt, but you have to do what's best for you.

Do you love and believe in the products? If you don't, people will see through that. And you'll give the signal that you're just all about the money.

First

Take massive action.

Don't wait until you feel that you have all the answers before you get started. So much of what you will learn will only be through direct, hands-on experience.

Network marketing trainer Jim Rohn had a great saying, "Leap and grow your wings on the way down." That's really the best way to get started.

You have to throw yourself into your new business. The good news is that you will have all the support you need to back you up. Massive action is prospecting, pointing them to a third-party tool, and plugging them into the already established system. If your lips are moving, you should be pointing to third-party tools.

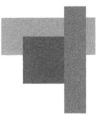

Randy Gage

❝ I don't need more money. I don't need more cars. I don't need more homes. I won't turn them away, but they don't drive me anymore. We all want success and the perks and toys that come with it.

But there's a much deeper level of satisfaction that comes with knowing you made a difference in the lives of the people on your team.

It's the personal breakthroughs of your people that move you from success to significance. That's what still drives me to this day. **❞**

Best

Seize the chance to be world-class.

Network marketing is the best business model in the world because it's the only one that really pays you exactly what you're worth, based exactly on the value that you create. That's either the scariest thing in the world to you or the most liberating thing.

Believe that you can create financial freedom, work at a world-class level, bring people into the business, nurture and guide them so that they can change the game for themselves, their own family, and the ones they love.

Reframe your mindset from a worrying, "Who can I get to sell this stuff?" to an empowered, "Who can I offer this opportunity to first?" Think to yourself, "I want out of the matrix, I'm going to reset my life and I'm going to go out and be amazing." You can do that the second you decide to become world-class.

Worst

Assume everyone is a leader.

When you go into meetings, you typically hear a speaker try to create excitement by yelling, "Everybody here's a leader! You wouldn't be here if you weren't a leader!" Well, that's ridiculous. Most people are there because they're living lives of quiet desperation. They're sick, broke, upset. Their life is miserable, and they're looking for a way out.

They're at the meeting because they know that twice a month they can be in the company of positive people. They're there because you serve donuts. Or someone praised them for the way they set up the product display, and no one praises them in any other aspect of their lives.

This is a wonderful group of people who are striving for something more in their lives, but they're not leaders yet. They're not willing to do the things that leadership requires. But maybe one day they will be.

We're driving a lot of amazing people out of the business by shoving leadership activity down their throats. They could have made that leap eventually, turned their lives around, changed the whole world for themselves and their families. But the pressure to turn them into leaders before they're ready drives them out of the business.

Give them the time they need to grow at their own pace. Love them. Offer them the pathway to leadership, so they know it's there when they're ready. Create a safe space for them where they belong and can appreciated for who they are at the moment.

When they're ready to step onto that safe pathway to leadership, they will.

First

Recruit, recruit, recruit.

During your first year in network marketing you need to be recruiting like crazy. You've got to go into high-level activity in how you recruit. Just get as many people exposed to your presentations as you can. Don't make it all about you. Don't even do a lot of one-on-ones. Use as many of the third-party tools as you can.

Your main priority is to be building your organization to the point where you have at least four well-developed lines in your downline chasing you, asking you to sit in on calls, inviting you to come meet them, meet new people four or five levels down from you. Your main job is to be in recruitment activity so much that your team builds to 40,000, 60,000 or 200,000 people. It's only at that point when you start thinking of yourself in leadership terms.

Once you get those four lines chasing you, you can take a break from recruiting and you can concentrate on driving depth and creating the team cultures that will help your team members recruit their own team members.

Eventually those lines will be so established you can start building new lines in a fresh round of recruiting. By that time you really start seeing results, it's easier to recruit, your group is growing and your check is growing. That's when it really becomes fun.

Puya Ghandian

" I don't look at network marketing as the chance to go
out there and move prod-
ucts. I look at it as an opportunity to help make people
better. Obviously the money
is exciting. The time freedom
is amazing. The lifestyle is
fantastic. And the oppor-
tunities that open to us are
great. But when you boil it
down to its core value, it's
about what you're able to
do for others. "

Best

Believe in yourself.

I find that with so many people it's not that they don't believe in the company. Nor do they doubt that success happens. Their problem is that they doubt themselves and the idea that they can go out and accomplish their dreams.

Give yourself permission to believe that you can do whatever you set your mind to over the next 90 days. That way you're allowing yourself to get out there, get your two exposures a day, and start bringing recruits in. All this will lead to confidence, which will help you keep believing in yourself.

The period of 90 days is a doable amount of time. People can do anything for 90 days. We all know that it takes 21 days to make or break a habit. So with 90 days your new habit of believing in yourself will have sunk in. You've created a new habit for yourself. You don't even have to commit beyond that point because believing in yourself will have become second nature.

Worst

Make a short-term commitment.

Stay for at least a year. That tenure will contribute to your belief. You'll have the chance to learn from your experience. You'll see first-hand why the do's work, and why the don'ts don't work. You'll also become known in your organization, and you'll be able to benefit from the relationships you'll build along the way.

Most importantly people you've shown the opportunity to early in your year will come to believe in you when they see that you're still in the business. You won't be able to recruit them if a year later they're ready but you're no longer active.

Recruiting is a process; it's not an event. So knowing you're committed to the business for at least a year takes the pressure off yourself to get people to say *yes* right off the bat. You're going into the conversation knowing that you have lots of time to enroll them. And if you allow them to go through the process of arriving to their *yes* in their own way, then that's meaningful to them.

If you give yourself at least a year, you give yourself the time to build and fill a pipeline of relationships in varying stages of the recruitment process. You don't have to treat everyone you meet as a potential sell. You can take the posture that says, "I don't need you in my business, even though I know you eventually will be." Think of it as a sort of anti-quantum leap. You can afford to take your time because you have given yourself the commitment of a year.

First

Reach out to your upline support.

Don't be shy to make sure your leadership knows who you are. You'd be surprised at how few people do that. But even though, as of this interview, my own organization is 20,000 people, if someone calls me, you bet they're going to get my attention.

Be specific about what your *whys* are, what goals you want to achieve and by when. Then do everything you say you're going to do, including do what your upline tells you to do. Do all the training they tell you to do and let them know as you do each task.

Your upline wants to see by your actions that you're serious about your business. As you go through the tasks your upline assigns you, you are proving that you're on the same page. And you'll get more and more of your upline's attention this way.

Kirk Gillespie

" I love being able to wake up every day knowing that I can build my own dream based on my values, my passion, the way I want to see my day unfold, and the people I want to be with. My efforts fulfill my own dream, not an employer's dream.

I can dream a big dream and know that I have the chance to make that dream come true. This is not just a business. It's a lifestyle that brings me joy, fulfillment, excitement, and, best of all, the chance to pass this way of living on to others. "

Best

Be good to yourself while learning.

You're going to be learning new habits and skills, in an entirely new business environment. There are going to be circumstances, challenges, and obstacles that you will be facing that will demand new ways of behaving and reacting. It's important that you manage your mindset during these times so that you are patient with yourself and keep your enthusiasm alive.

Always keep in mind that you already have everything you need to be great at this business. It's not a matter of being able to control everything. It's a matter of deciding how you're going to react to what happens to you. And even that's a skill that you have to learn – controlling how you react to an unfamiliar situation and choosing a positive mindset, even when you're feeling overwhelmed and scared. Give yourself permission to be kind to yourself while you learn it.

Worst

Undermine your positive mindset.

When we come into this business, we bring committees with us – our friends, relatives, even our own self-talk – who love to be judgmental and doubtful. They tell us we're not worthy or deserving or able.

Usually our own inner voice is the loudest. People start this business with all kinds of internal critics, with all kinds of mindsets that they've been brought up with. There's a whole library of negative self-talk that just takes time to dismantle. But you can do it. You can refocus. You don't have to listen to the voices you've been used to hearing up until this point.

This principle goes for other people too. Don't share your new dream with people who you already know are toxic to your spirit. They don't have to understand your business or approve of it before you can commit to it yourself. Develop a circle of friends who love you enough to be able to say, "I don't quite understand what you're up to, but I believe you can do anything you want to. And I'm right with you, cheering you on."

First

Prepare for challenging times.

Give yourself positive influences and information sources that you can pour yourself into. Get a list of books and training CDs that will help you begin changing the way you've been thinking toward a more positive, self-empowered outlook.

Identify the way you've been relieving stress and anxiety in the past and develop healthier habits. Make a list of things you can do instead of reaching for chocolate, alcohol, or unhealthy foods: Take a walk, take a bath, call a friend, go to a movie – whatever takes you out of the grip of negative thinking.

Take a 30-day break from influences that trigger negative or stressful thoughts. Notice specifically what drains your positivity and energy and see if you can remove those elements from your life – even if for only 30 days. You don't have to make a permanent break – which is hard to do anyway, especially if one of those triggers is a family member.

Also build a daily discipline to program your subconscious to be more positive and empowered. It's one of the most important disciplines that anyone who has their own business can adopt. Write in a gratitude journal as part of your morning routine. When you focus on what you're grateful for, it's really hard to start a downward spiral of a bad mood or negativity.

Above all, start your day with the mental vision of what you want the end of the day to look like. When all is said and done, what do you want to be celebrating tonight?

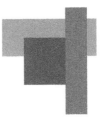

Amee Gleave

" The reward is really the people you meet in this business; the friendships you make. I could never imagine having such inspiring friends in my life – who I look up to, who I aspire to be like. It would have never come into my life without network marketing. "

Best

Remember the importance of people.

Success comes when you focus on helping others get what they want. But we tend to forget that. We are so excited about our products and opportunity that we don't listen to what our prospects need. We make the mistake of saying, "I love it because it did this and this and this." Or, "Oh my gosh! You've got to try this! It's going to make your back ache go away," when all your prospects may really want is to lose a little weight or feel better in a general way.

You've got to listen. Too many of us think that "listening" is just being quiet until it's our turn to speak. When we really know what other people's pains and needs are, we will then know what specific solution we have to offer them. But we get so excited about our offerings that we forget to focus on what others specifically need.

Sometimes what they need is just a kind word in passing. The other day, I complimented a woman I didn't know on her beautiful hair. By the way she reacted, you'd think that one little compliment changed her life. We need to do that kind of thing more.

Worst

Disrespect your energy bank.

We're influenced positively or negatively by the people we hang out with. Are you surrounding yourself with victims or with victors? One minute you are talking to a highly successful, inspiring network marketer and you think, "Wow! This is something I have to do!" But then the next minute you're talking to your self-pitying best friend or uncle who has never made much of his life. It's so hard to prevent that kind of person from infecting your brain with doubt. Don't listen to people who don't have what you want or who are not going where you're going.

Know who the negative influences are in your life. I'm not saying you need to get rid of your best friend, or sister, or spouse. But just know which people drain your energy and which ones fill you up.

Think of it this way: We each have an energy bank. When we wake up in the morning it's 100% full. Then as we go through the day every single person we come into contact with is either feeding it, helping us toward our goals and dreams, or robbing from it with their drama, negativity, or self-pity.

I was getting a lot of people like that in my life. Then one day someone said to me, "The most important people in your life are your husband and daughters, right?" "Absolutely," I said. "Would you do anything for them?" "You name it," I said.

And then she said, "Would you manage your energy bank differently if you knew that when they got home at the end of the day you were only going to be at 20%?"

That's what caused a major shift in the way I manage my day and whom I interact with. From that point on I've protected my energy bank because I'm protecting it for my family. I want to be at least 80% or 90% when they walk in the door at the end of the day.

First

Commit to sticking with your business.

You don't start a marriage with the idea of trying it for 18 days and then quitting when it gets too hard. Neither should you start this business with that attitude.

Look for role models of people who have succeeded over time despite their failures. My favorite is Michael Jordan. He missed over 9,000 shots in his career; 26 of those shots would have been game-winning shots. His team lost almost 300 games. But he's still one of the most successful basketball players in history.

Most people have the mentality that they just want all their success to happen right away. But it's really a two- to four-year plan. If you don't quit, if you stay in action and remain coachable, your success is inevitable.

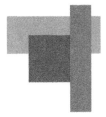

Natalie Goddard

" I stay passionate about network marketing because of the joy that comes with each connection I make. For me network marketing is about bringing hope to every home. And when I see hope come alive in people, there's nothing like it. When I see that fire in their eyes, I know they understand the possibility of where they can go and how network marketing can shift their life. I'm addicted to that feeling. "

Best

Connect powerfully.

Connect with your Higher Power so that you will be guided in your efforts. I've seen people attracted to network marketing because of the hope that it will remove them from the rat race. But if you're not guided in your efforts, you will be in a rat race even more than ever.

I've seen people enrolling, enrolling, and enrolling, but they haven't found the right leaders yet because they haven't taken the time to connect with their Higher Power.

Next, connect deeply with others. Create massive value for them in that moment, even if it's just carefully listening so that you can offer a solution you've experienced. When I think of people I would go anywhere with and do anything for, they are the people who would look me in the eye and truly connect to my heart and soul. We see and care about each other for who we are. Those connections don't go away. Those are the leaders you want to work with for the next 40 to 50 years.

Worst

Go into this business half-heartedly.

Any way that you're holding back means that you're not all in. Maybe you're waiting for a better company that you think is just around the corner. Or there are certain categories of people you don't want to share the business with – like your closest friends and family. If you're not sharing your opportunity with everyone you know, that's an indication that you're still split. If you don't put your heart into this, you might as well not do anything at all. People will pick up on your inauthenticity.

You have to be all in. That way, your only option is absolute success. And you'll attract leaders who have the confidence in you to go all in themselves.

First

Find the opportunity that fits.

Finding the right match with a network marketing opportunity is like finding the right spouse. When you connect to the right match, you have an amazing vehicle to create something together powerfully. If you try to make something fit, but it really doesn't align with your gifts, talents, energy and passion, you're trying too hard. You're starting without flow.

Find an opportunity that matches you so you start in flow from the beginning. You're aligning with a passion that's already within you. It's what I call *authentic network marketing*. It's network marketing that flows. It's natural, it's real. There doesn't need to be pretense. There are no masks.

Find a product that you can believe in. And that belief grows. Then believe in the company, the opportunity that the company offers and its leadership. Then you can focus your efforts on developing yourself and sharing powerfully with others.

Have both eyes open when choosing a sponsor. You need a sponsor who is aligned with your values and your passions. You need a sponsor who is committed to helping you grow into your best self – authentically. If it's not your immediate sponsor who represents those advantages for you, find someone in your upline whom you can align with and who will support you.

When you have those fundamentals in place, then you can learn the other components essential to your success.

Remember the power of your own authenticity. Even if the company, the product, and sponsor are great, if you're fake, you'll continue to search for success.

Choose to do authentic network marketing, and success will flow to you.

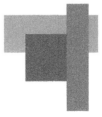

Debi Granite

" Prepare to be surprised at yourself as you discover the inner leader within that you didn't even know existed. We're all exceptional and born for greatness. And network marketing may be the first opportunity you have had to tap into the identity of how big you really are and what wonderful things you are really capable of. You will be amazed at your new powers! "

Best

Break your own sound barrier.

No matter who you were before you started network marketing, you will grow and break through your preconceived boundaries as you discover new personal powers in this business.

To be successful in network marketing, you'll be tapping into unknown wells of potential and resourcefulness. You're going to be learning how to motivate, how to inspire, even how to ignite a passion for higher performance standards in your team.

And you're going to be making a lot of noise as you grow and pick up speed in your team-building. A lot of people feel fear as they grow into their new leadership levels, even if they're a natural-born leader. You will be helping your team members grow into their new leadership roles. That's where your success will ultimately lie – helping others. But first you have to come to grips with the new version of you that you are becoming.

Will you like yourself as you take the necessary actions to bring your teams into the success they deserve? Will your family accept the new you? Are you going to have to abandon your old role at home, which could upset people who have counted on you to stay in your box? Will you be able to gracefully apologize when you try a new leadership skill and mess up at first? Will you be able to forgive yourself?

Hear that boom? That's you breaking your own sound barrier. That's you growing, growing out of your comfort zone. Anyone who has heard a sonic boom knows that it's scary and often unexpected. But all that noise is just you busting through preconceived limitations of who you are and what you're capable of.

Worst

Behave like an office barracuda.

If you come to network marketing after having worked in a traditional corporate environment for several years, you will probably have some old habits, behaviors, and beliefs to unravel. In the traditional corporate situation, people succeed by winning in competitive environments where someone else must lose. But in network marketing, you succeed by helping others succeed. In fact that's the only way you can succeed.

My short journey into the corporate world was brutal. When my boss's administrative assistant in my first job decided she didn't like someone, she made sure they suffered. I was the fourth person within a single year to get fired. In my second job I discovered that the key to success in that culture was to bow down to a pecking order and play office politics. That's just an unhealthy way for me to live.

Whether you were on the receiving end of an office barracuda's meanness or you were the office barracuda yourself, network marketing offers you a wonderful way to heal.

Check your guns at the door, so to speak. Abandon your attachment to political intrigue. It doesn't have any place in network marketing. And if you find yourself in a team where some of that is going on, remember that you are the leader of your own team culture. You are the leader of your own tribe. Make it one that thrives on trust and mutual support.

First

Give yourself time off.

Network marketing is so all-encompassing that it's hard to turn it off. After all, that person on the sticky mat next to you in the yoga class could be The One, right? How can you expect to go to yoga to totally unplug? Well you have to. Otherwise you'll burn out, and you'll lose out on the other joys of life.

Reserve a certain amount of time every week to do the things you love that have nothing to do with network marketing. Turn off the phone. And just be present to the people and activities you love for their own sake.

Justin Harrison

" For me, the reward of network marketing is the joy of watching people reach their true potential – seeing people who were making minimum wage now making $20,000 a month. And it's not just financial benefit – that's awesome too – but the best thing is seeing the changes in who they become as a person. "

Best

Build teams that thrive on learning.

From the very beginning of your career in network marketing, commit to the ideal of creating teams of partners who recognize the essential value of learning. And that includes being active participants in teaching each other, as well.

In my company we have a program that encourages our leaders to dedicate some of their time traveling the country and teaching our distributors – even people who are in others' organizations. It's an essential part of who we are. And we proudly fill our corporate calendar with events that are open to our distributors from coast to coast.

Of course, it's easier if you are associated with a company that supports this learning on a national level. But you can take control over your own team's learning culture even without support from your company. There's nothing stopping you from taking that initiative.

Even if you're still operating on a local level, you can share your teaching responsibilities with your more experienced, informed, or enthusiastic team members. Encourage and support members who want to learn how to teach by giving them the opportunity to run a call or a weekly meeting. By learning to teach, they're also learning to learn. So because they're helping your larger organization grow and develop, they're developing to their own next level themselves.

Be the team that attracts people who are excited to teach and learn. Prospect new team members in learning environments, like community college extension classes, where the learning is elective. Prospect the teachers. You'd be surprised how many of these teachers are professionals during the day, and are teaching at night as a way to raise a second income.

Worst

Overload your people.

It's important to build a culture that promotes learning and personal development. But if you overload your people with too many books to read or lots of long video trainings to watch, you will risk that possibility that some will spend all their time training instead of going out and building their business. A half hour dedicated to reading every day is more than awesome.

I'm also finding that the long videos aren't effective anymore. People just don't want to watch 60-minute classes. We live in a chronically ADD culture. Instead of doing a full 45 minutes or an hour, do four 10-minute videos – or even shorter, if you can.

First

Create a basic curriculum.

When people are really ready to get involved in the business – as opposed to being wholesale customers, which every company needs – give them a "check up from the neck up," as Zig Zigler said. Give them the assignment to read a core group of books that you believe will support their business and growth.

This assignment will also help you see who is going to be serious about their business. If they actually read the books you recommend, you'll be able to identify them as the ones most likely to take action and own their success.

For my group, we always start our people out with Randy Gage's *Making the First Circle Work*, Michael Clouse's *Learning the Business One Story at a Time*, and Jeff Olson's *The Slight Edge*. I think *The Slight Edge* is one of the best books ever written. Everyone should read it regardless of what they do in life.

This has been huge for us because we live in a super negative culture. Starting everyone with these three books helps people get out of that mire of negative ooze that everyone seems to be trapped in.

Ray Higdon

" I love network marketing in that it is totally and wholly attached to how many people you can help. I wake up every day and get emails from people around the world who have gotten some benefit from my influence – they've grown their team, they are able to retire their parents, they've improved their own health. Those kinds of stories get me fired up. "

Best

Be patient.

It's so common in our profession to shine the spotlight on major success stories – seemingly overnight success stories. And, naturally, people get frustrated. They look at their own efforts and wonder, "What's wrong with me? What am I doing wrong?" But you have to understand that overnight success takes time. People may tell you that they recruited 30 people in the "first" month. But they don't tell you about all those months of effort leading up to that "first" month. You don't hear about all those months of building their brands; building their list and developing a following; figuring out the various systems that will ultimately get them to that "overnight" success story.

When you're beginning to build the online side of your business, the key is to keep consistently putting out value into the marketplace so that you will eventually attract more and more people to you. And if you're going to commit to this, you also need to commit to doing it for a period of time – at least six months. In the meantime, actively prospect in more conventional ways.

Worst

Feel like you must be a tech expert.

If you're starting your online marketing now, you're coming into it at a very good time. You don't have to be super-technical if you want to do a lot of it yourself. But better yet, it's really inexpensive to outsource the components of the work that you don't want to do. Why spend your time learning skills that aren't directly income-producing?

I've seen way too many people get so bogged down with learning code, how to create an opt-in page, or building a website that they just get frustrated and quit. Or let's say they push through their frustration, and invest six to eight hours into their project. But the result isn't perfect or polished. And then they quit. Just think, they could have spent all that time on business-building activities. Outsource those things.

The only online activities you should not outsource is your content creation: Your blogs and social media inter-actions. Those are your customer touchpoints – your op-portunities to develop your brand and reputation. Those are your chances to build relationships and learn who your customers are and what they want. Don't outsource the pieces that can only be uniquely you.

First

Know who your target audience is.

It's said that anybody can be in network marketing. If that's the case, why not pick the prospect who is perfect for you? Who would you love to go on vacations with? Have long conversations with? Stay up late at night and share stories with? What are their hobbies and profes-sions? The more specific you are regarding the kinds of people you would want in your teams, the more effective your recruiting and marketing messages will be. Then you can craft all your messages to be congruent with attract-ing these people. You will be able to express yourself in a way that your target audience will say, "Man! It was like you were speaking directly to me! It was like you were reading my mind."

When you approach your blogging efforts with that in mind, you'll be asking yourself what messages will most resonate with the people you want to reach. That's a much more satisfying focus than worrying about how many eyeballs will see your site that day.

David Hsiung

" Network marketing gives us the rare chance to offer a solution to an immediate problem, and then follow up with an opportunity to change people's lives financially.

One of my team members was a shy musician with debilitating arthritis. She tried everything, including surgery. When I introduced her to the product, she found more than relief from her pain, she found a new business. She is now an inspiring leader. And makes five times more than she did as a renowned musician. "

Best

Make learning your top priority.

Dedicate 90% of your time to learning the business. I know you're so excited that you'll want to talk to your friends and family about your new discovery right away. But that time will come. You only have so many close relationships, you want to take very good care of them. You certainly don't want to learn on them and risk straining those relationships.

Most companies have very well developed learning channels online: Facebook, Twitter, online training videos housed on their websites, Youtube channels, your own sponsor's website. Get a comprehensive understanding of what's available to you. And take advantage of the fact that you can tap into them 24 hours a day, no matter where you are in the world. This is especially important if you want to grow an international business.

Understanding the array of learning opportunities that are available to you will also help you explain those resources to the people you sponsor. Make sure that you incorporate these online programs into your own team training.

Worst

Think going international is easy.

People tend to underestimate the difficulty and complexity in going international. If you don't do it right, you will waste a lot of money and time flying all over the world trying to open new markets.

You need to be strategic when you decide to target an international market. Develop an expertise in building your business locally first. Learn as much as you can about the business, the product, network marketing, and entrepreneurialism before you even start to think about taking your business beyond your own country's borders into new cultures and economies.

First

Choose business-friendly countries.

When you do decide that you're ready to go international, there are multiple ways to lower the barrier to entry for yourself and your organization. The first thing is to choose countries where you will be most likely to succeed.

The first thing to do is identify which countries already have an established relationship with your company. Your company has met the legal requirements to have a presence there. And your company already has a system in place to support your business growth efforts in the countries of your choice.

Secondly, choose destinations that support entrepreneurialism as a cultural value. Throughout Asia almost everyone has the dream to own their own business, largely because there aren't enough large companies located there to hire everyone who needs an income. So small businesses are normal there. When I was growing up in China, every mom in every house was handmaking something to sell. It's our way of life here. You will meet plenty of people who are receptive to hearing about network marketing, simply because there have never been enough jobs to go around.

Finally, start growing your business with at least one relationship with someone already living there. If you grow your organization based on relationships that are already in place, your people will be much more committed to succeed. It's all about deep, trusted relationships.

Put the right leaders in place at the very beginning – people who have a network of loyal friends and family who trust them – and that team will be a long-lasting one. It's all about the relationships.

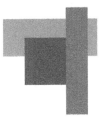

Donna Imson

" Network marketing has done so much for me and my family, people I know, and even people I've never met who are in my organization. I had amazing role models and sources of inspiration from so many different people. At the same time, there are still so many more people out there whose lives can change because of what we do. It's an opportunity to pay it forward. "

Best

Have a healthy relationship with *no*.

I learned to treat the word *no* not as a flat rejection but as an invitation to learn something new. I don't believe in coincidences. So I trust that with that *no* there is an important message. So when I hear *no*, I think, "There must be a reason I'm getting this *no*. What do I need to change? How could I do better next time? What do I need to improve?"

We build a healthy relationship by taking on the pain of the rejection and feeling it fully. Pain is good. It tells us what needs to be changed. By actually feeling the pain of the rejection, you'll be more likely to get the answers to the question, "Okay, what do I need to do because I don't want to feel this pain again?"

This is where the importance of perspective comes in. Setting your eyes on the prize, keeping a view to the long-term goals and holding onto the belief that there is a future in all this effort – all those mental disciplines will support you when you're first getting started in network marketing.

Eventually someone will say *yes* to you. And that will do wonders to your confidence, belief in the business, and faith in your vision. But before you get to that first *yes*, you struggle with the word *no*.

Worst

Say *yes* to your fears of rejection.

Brian Klemmer said, "Your greatest intent will always win." When I started out, I was very afraid of being rejected. And avoiding rejection could have been my greatest intent if I let it. But that fear was superseded by a greater intent – to give my children the best life that I could. I still felt the pain of rejection. I still felt afraid to approach people about the business. But I stopped allowing that fear to be debilitating.

So instead of saying *yes* to my fears, I was actually saying *no*. I had to say *no* to all those bad habits that I created, all those walls I built to protect myself from rejection. Those fears had become such a part of me, I was actually saying *no* to myself – saying *no* to the fear itself and to the effect of the fear.

I still took the rejections hard. They still hurt. But by refusing to take on those fears, I eventually built the skills to say *no* to the hurt and consciously set it aside. That way I could keep moving on.

First

Make your *why* stronger than fear.

You can have all sorts of terrible fears around rejection, but they won't matter if you've got a strong *why*. That strong *why* will give you the courage to develop that healthy relationship with the word *no*. It will give you that sense of perspective and proportion to face the hurt and keep moving forward.

Your success is determined by your daily agenda. Every day you have to say *no* to your limited beliefs and the moment-by-moment excuses not to work your business. On a daily basis, tap into that strong *why*, and nurture it so that it continues to get stronger.

Make sure your daily agenda includes time for renewing your mind, strengthening your beliefs in yourself and the business, and detoxifying your emotions. That will make your *why* always more powerful than your fear of rejection.

Lisa Jimenez

" I love network marketing because of who we can become with this business model. Everyone starts at the same place. You have to buy a starter pack, you have to inspire and educate people on your prospect list. You have to encourage, and coach, and lead them.

And who do you become as a result? A leader. A contributor to the planet. You create a space for others' greatness, a realm of trust, community, family, love, connection. There's no greater gift than that. "

Best
Change the way you see yourself.

You can never out-succeed your self-view. If you don't see yourself as a successful network marketer, a knock-out presenter, a multi-millionaire, and the leader of an empire, you can't create it.

When you transform your self-view, you help overcome your self-sabotage – that inner voice that says, "You're not all that. You're not really good at this." "You don't know what you're doing." "Someone said *no* to you again. See? You're no good at this."

That voice is normal. The way to deal with the gap between who you are now and who you're becoming is to take on the posture of the person you want to become. Keep saying to yourself, "I'm a brilliant presenter." "People love what I have to say." "People want to come into my business." This all subconsciously helps to transform your self-view.

We've got to keep telling ourselves these things because everything and everyone is telling us the opposite.

Worst
Listen to reality.

This is the time when you need to build your beliefs in the face of contradicting evidence. You've got to be willing to believe in the fantasy more than you believe in the reality. And you have to protect your dream with all your heart.

When you're first starting out, the roots of your beliefs are very weak. People can pull them out of the ground so easily because your roots have not had enough time to create the deep connection with the soil, conviction, and belief that success can happen for you.

You can't let reality have the last word during this time. Build daily habits to reinforce that fantasy in your mind. Take 20 minutes to an hour to pray, meditate, visualize your fantasy as though it's real. Find people who have already created what you want to create and emulate them. Study what they did, their way of being, their habits, and their characteristics.

Focusing on your fantasy will give you the clarity you need to grow into your new self. And clarity is power. You will give your reticular activating system the picture, the destination, the image, the exact address of where you want to end up. That new home. That bonus check. That commission check. That team with all those wonderful people in your organization.

Success is created in your mind first. Focus on that instead of reality.

First

Make friends with fear.

Fear is normal. When you experience fear, it's a clue that you're on to something big. It means that you've got a God-sized dream. It's a sign that you're on the right track. Even though we're taught as children that fear is a self-preservation mechanism, when it comes to growing yourself into amazing success, learn to regard fear as your green light to go.

So welcome it as an old friend when it appears in your life. The way to befriend fear is to neutralize its effects with its opposite – faith. Faith in your new self-view. Faith in the comp plan. Faith in the product line. Faith that you're divinely guided and that what you want wants you.

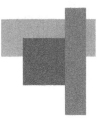

Donna Johnson

" Staying motivated has a lot to do with your drive, your passion, your *why*. You need to be setting the next goals. And those goals turn from practical goals to more significant and meaningful goals.

When I started imagining what I could do with six figures every month, I was traveling to Africa and India. And I was seeing the need there. So it got me excited to realize that if I made more money, I could help more people. "

Best

Just go all in.

If you commit to going all in, dedicating yourself to the business, and managing your expectations, you will see the results you are looking for. Commit – and don't just commit half-heartedly. Most people overestimate what they can do in a year, but they underestimate what they can do in five years.

You have to understand that it's not like a traditional job where you're trading hours for dollars immediately. It's like building a skyscraper. Things are going to be happening underground for a while before you see the building pop up.

So you need to match your go-all-in enthusiasm with patience, focus, and a tolerance for delayed gratification. I've noticed especially in the last decade or so that people's attention span has decreased. They get restless and they want their rewards now.

Going all in means not only total commitment to your new business but also disciplining yourself to understand and manage your expectations.

Go all in and don't do it half-heartedly.

Worst

Launch yourself the wrong way.

You want to feel small successes along the way. This approach builds your self-esteem, confidence, and beliefs as you watch your paycheck grow. But two things commonly hold people back when they start:

They think that they have to get their PhD in the business before they go out and start inviting people to look at the opportunity. They spend their time reading, studying, and Googling when they should be out meeting with people.

Or they completely ignore the system and jump in blindly. They just spin their wheels with excitement but never get any forward traction. The fresh excitement is good but you still have to plug into the system so you can learn how to make your first few presentations and appointments productive. That gets you started in the right direction.

First
Get into activity with the system.

Don't even wait for your starter kit to come in before you get busy. When I sponsor someone new, I have three activities: I introduce them to the system; I reaffirm the wisdom of the decision that they've made; I remind them that they will be duplicating what you're teaching them.

One of the most important lessons that you will be modeling for your team is the experience of launching and relaunching yourself with each new level of achievement that you attain. There will be times when you hit plateaus or reach a major objective. That's when you get into activity all over again, freshly with a new burst of speed and inspiration.

At each new level you'll be seeing for yourself a whole new set of possibilities that will come as a result of your success. All those people who are watching you take on this new challenge will be inspired to get into a resurgence of activity themselves.

There may come a time when you've reached an income level that is beyond anything you ever expected. And you'll be tempted to ask yourself, "Who am I to be making this much money?" Just remember that the only reason you're making a lot of money is because you're helping other people achieve their money objectives. So who are you to hold them back?

Whether you're just starting out or you've achieved that beyond-your-wildest-dreams objective, it's time to get back into activity with the system. And show your organization what's possible for them too.

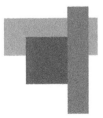

Art Jonak

" Network marketing is an amazing avenue for finding mentors who care about you because your success is their success. It can help reignite your dreams for yourself and your family.

Even while you pursue those dreams, you'll be learning skills that will equip you to go and help thousands of other people. And all along the way, you'll learn some amazing things about yourself. "

Best

Lead with love.

One of the best feelings in the world is knowing you actually mean something to someone, having a friend who helps you up when you fall and who also celebrates your victories – that special person who believes in your dreams.

When I joined network marketing, I was told to "lead with the money!" Over time I learned what truly grows and bonds a team was leading with compassion, leading with love. When you lead with love, people will open up and share their dreams. And that fires me up, because I know, through that dream, I can teach them principles they can use for the rest of their lives.

People are going to stumble and fall, they will disappoint us, they'll even stop believing in themselves, but we have to believe in them anyway. The moment we lose belief in people, and in their dreams, is the moment we're out of business.

Each of us has a responsibility to ourselves and to our families to move in the direction of our dreams. Support those dreams by surrounding yourself and your team with positivity, caring, understanding, and compassion. In fact, take that love beyond your team and extend it to everyone in your company... extend it to the entire profession of network marketing. And beyond that to people outside of the profession. Even if they don't join us, love on them.

Worst

Be a know-it-all.

When I first got involved, I was a know-it-all. No question about it. I didn't listen to my sponsors. They were all older than me, and I thought, "These guys are dinosaurs. I'm smarter. I can do this without their help." You can do it yourself and waste a lot of time trying and failing at techniques that have already been tried and discarded. Or you can pick up ideas and skills directly from people who have already done it successfully.

Of course, there are always exceptions to this rule. But my advice is to become what I call, "hone-able." No matter how long you've been in network marketing, there is always a lot to learn, and it's much easier to learn it from other people's experiences where possible.

This is especially important, given the nature of our profession. In our case, it's not just about what works – which would be the case if you were learning how to be a doctor, lawyer, or accountant. It's about what duplicates. The best place to get that information is from people who have been successful inside the network marketing profession before you.

First

Be the project.

A successful life begins with the assumption that you will be successful. Knowing this, you realize no compensation plan, product, or sponsor will get you there. Ultimately it's going to be you who has to get you there. This takes away a lot of external pressures while creating positive pressure on yourself to become better. That's part of the goal, to always get better.

You become the project. You'll strive to close the gap between who you are now and who you need to be once you've achieved that success. When you wake up in the morning, your top goal will be, "How can I get better today?"

When things don't go the way you want, it's best to just accept the result, learn from it, adjust, and move forward. Stop trying to get out of the work. Do the work. When you look at who is successful, they've all put in the work. They worked harder on themselves than anything else. Why? They know what you will soon find out for yourself: The harder you fight for something, the more you'll value it once you achieve it, the more you'll fight to protect it, and most importantly the greater you'll have become as a result of it.

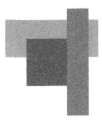

Michelle Jones

" Network marketing is about helping others and changing lives. Shift the focus from your own recruiting agenda to an attitude of, 'I'm here to serve those who are looking for something more,' and that's where you'll find the source of your own lasting success. In the traditional business world, it's you against 'them.' But in this profession, the faster you grasp that it's about helping others, the quicker you're going to grow. "

Best

Remember that everyone is different.

Typically in our profession we hear the stories of the cars, the trips, and the six-figure incomes. But think about all the other people out there who are looking for just an extra $500 or $1,000 a month that would dramatically change their lives. It's about helping that one person reduce their work load, or getting that one person to the point where she can stay home an extra day with her child. Or helping a couple pay off their credit card or electric bill.

The big stories are great. But the smaller stories will get you further. When you're sharing that Susie on your team was able to pay off her child's braces. Or Mary was able to pay off her debts; that is more real to the majority of the people you introduce the business to.

Worst

Assume all are motivated by money.

There are so many people who are already happy with what they have financially. Once, earlier in my career, I went to an event where someone tried to get the room fired up with enthusiasm by saying, "Everyone who would want $1,000 a month more, stand up!" And one woman said, "Actually, I'm fine financially." It turns out that she was passionate about giving back to her church and community. So we helped her see that if she had more, she would be able to give more.

The emphasis on money turns a lot of people off to network marketing. Everyone needs something more, but it's not always going to be about money. For me, I needed more time freedom. For others, it's about more happiness in their lives or a sense of life purpose. Or they want to belong to a community of positive, happy people.

First

Discover what your prospects want.

When you're meeting with anyone, take the time to find out what it is that they want more of in life. When you figure that out, just put them on that path to get it. That's where your success is going to come from.

Everyone in this profession has their ups and downs – just like with any career. But when you're in business for yours – and your business is to lift other people up – it's all the more important to ride out those down times. And it's important to help your team members ride theirs out too. When you know their *why*, you can remind them of it in vivid, powerful terms. That's your most powerful tool for helping your team members get back on track more quickly.

This way you can help them stay motivated in ways that are most relevant to them. And you will know when they have achieved their *why*. That's when you'll start compiling some great stories that will inspire and motivate your team members and prospects.

It all comes down to having more options. If you have more options, you can help more people. Outside of network marketing, people get on this wheel of life: They get up, they go to work, and they come home too tired to enjoy their families. They work all year for that vacation. But then they're too exhausted to enjoy it.

I want people on my team who just want something more. But I have to take the time to find out specifically what that more is. Only then can I really help them. When they can use this profession to get what they want, they can then share their stories to attract more people who want more. And then, in turn, help them get it. That's what network marketing is really about.

Kimber King

" Every morning I wake up feeling super blessed that I can design my own day. If my children need me, or if my husband suddenly says, 'Let's drive to San Diego,' I can be there for them.

I have time and financial freedom. I want to give other people the chance to design their own days exactly the way they want to. That's the kind of freedom this business brings to the world. "

Best

Work in short bursts of time.

All of us are surrounded by constant and competing demands for our time, attention, and energy. When we're with our family, we worry that we're not growing our business. When we're working, we feel guilty that we're not with our precious family. And even when we do sit down at our desk, then we're torn between focusing on our work, email, Facebook, and messages that keep coming in.

By systematically approaching your business in terms of short, defined periods of time, you're giving yourself permission to focus only on that for, say, 50 minutes at a time. Assuming, of course, that your children are safe and taken care of during that time, you can push any other distractions to the side for 50 minutes. Then you know that you can take a 10-minute break to catch up on the more urgent emails and Facebook posts. Then you can return refreshed to another block of 50 minutes, giving yourself permission to focus on your work again.

This way you are giving yourself the gift of undivided attention. We all know that guilty feeling that we're not focusing on something or someone who needs or wants us. But by defining these bursts of time to focus on only one thing at a time, you can do your work without as much stress.

The ultimate gift to yourself is the peace of mind you have knowing that each person in your life and each component of your life are getting the attention from you that they deserve.

Worst

Think that you have to do it all.

When you bring a new person into your organization, you're also bringing in a whole new set of talents, skills, and passions that will enrich the abilities of your entire group. And make your own life easier. While everyone needs to be able to do the basics, wouldn't it be great to know that you have someone on the team who just loves doing three-way calls? Or that here's someone on your team who is an organization expert? Or who loves helping out with home parties?

In addition to growing their own individual businesses, your team members can support each other across lines. It's all about collaboration these days. Look for complimentary talents and gifts in your team and put those people together for mutual support.

First

Be passionate about the product.

When I started in this business, I was so excited about the product that I knew people would benefit from using it. My own results were obvious. So my business grew fast that way.

So many people feel that they have to wait until they know everything about the business and have all the recruitment skills down before they have the nerve to step out and try to build their business. But when you're authentically passionate about the benefits you get just from using the product or service, people will be naturally drawn to you.

Just love the product or service, don't worry about things like formulations. Most people want to know: Did it work for you? Is it safe? Can I get my money back if it doesn't work for me?

Know just enough about your product to be passionate about it on the level of the consumer experience. For that small percentage who want to know the details, point them to the information tools your company provides.

Becca Levie

" We think we're hungry just to pay the bills. But really, we're hungry to believe in ourselves. To be satisfied and content. And to have our lives full of wonderful relationships.

When you first step into the shoes of this profession, they're going to pinch and feel uncomfortable. But if you keep walking in them, and stay connected to those who have brought you into this opportunity, eventually those shoes are going to get very comfortable. And one day you will say, 'I had no idea that life could feel so good.' "

Best

Look for role models.

Start going to events and listening in on teleconferences. What you're looking for is a group of people who are experiencing the same kind of success you want to experience. When you listen to their stories, you'll be able to think to yourself, "Well, if so-and-so did this, I can do it too. They have nothing different than what I'm being offered. I have the same products, the same pricing, and the same compensation plan. They obviously got *nos* too. But they didn't stop there. They continued forward until they got all the *yeses* to get all the great things our profession offers."

In looking for a mentor, don't just focus on the stars on the stage. Find people in the audience who stand out to you for their positivity or energy, or whatever it is that makes them sparkle. Get their business cards and contact them. Every little bit of wisdom moves you forward.

No matter where you are in your business, you can start building a community of people who are just a little more advanced than you are so you have something to aspire to. You just need to expose yourself to their example, experiences, and advice.

Worst

Fail to protect your dream.

Don't forget that spark, that excitement, that electricity, that caused you to get passionate about this new journey that will take your life to the next level.

You're going to face negativity and false little messages that tell you that what you want isn't possible. So you have to remember to protect the vision of what you want for yourself. And remain plugged into that electrical charge that you had the moment you said, "I'm going to do something different with my world."

Protect that feeling with everything you've got. There will be times when your light is burning brightly but then someone comes along and unplugs you from that electrical charge, even for just a moment. They reject your opportunity. Or they criticize your dreams. What can you do? Don't engage in a battle of perceptions. Sometimes it's best to just say to the person, "Thank you for sharing," but in your mind, say, "Next!"

That person may not understand what you have to offer now. But maybe they will later. In the meantime, you have to protect your own light and vision.

Remember that there are millions of people out there, and certainly many of them want to have what you have to offer. There's absolutely no doubt about it. So protect yourself and move quickly through the others.

First

Aim for 10 *yeses* as your first goal.

Ten is a number that everyone can be comfortable with. It's a short sprint, but it's also within our reach psychologically. So we can aim for going out and getting those 10 *yeses*. If we've already got the mindset that we're not going to argue and battle our way, we're simply going to quickly find those people who want what we have.

My approach is holding the belief that anyone I come into contact throughout the day is there for a reason. There's a purpose to my life. And I want to share my gifts.

Now, are they going to be ready to accept my gift in that moment? Maybe yes, maybe no. Maybe they will eventually, through five to eight exposures along the way. So I'm not going to spend hours or a whole day on one person, giving them my time and power if they don't want what I have right away. That's why it's important to remember the goal of 10 *yeses* and keep the momentum going.

Tracy Monteforte

" People make money. But systems generate wealth. When you have a system, with a set of daily activities and tools to support your process, then you can generate serious wealth.

Nothing is left to 'by guess and by golly.' Systems are essential because they keep you on track and focused on what makes you money. "

Best

Listen authentically.

The American psychologist, Milton Erickson, once said, "Anything is possible in the presence of a good rapport." What is rapport? Rapport is trust and a sense of emotional affinity. When you are prospecting people you don't know yet to build your team, you must establish rapport quickly. Then they will see that you have their best interests at heart and in mind. And then they'll be open to whatever you have to offer to them.

To achieve that emotional affinity, you have to put your own agenda aside, as you're having your initial conversations with them. Don't be so wrapped up in what you're going to say next to them that you completely miss what they're saying to you.

Listen carefully to what they're saying to you, and you will find that they're giving you all the clues you need to present your opportunity in a way that appeals specifically and directly to them.

Worst

Depend too much on your script.

When you use a well-written, tested and proven script, you can establish rapport within seven seconds. That's how valuable the right script can be.

But when you depend too much on the script -- focusing on what the script is telling you to say next, instead of paying attention to the person you're talking to, you can lose that rapport in an instant.

You may have the script, but the person you're talking to doesn't. So they may answer your questions out of order. If you ask them why they're looking for a home-based income, and they say that they just got laid off, then obviously don't ask them what their current job is, even though that's the next question on your script.

We all know what it feels like to talk to a customer support rep who is chained to a script. Don't be one of those people. Use a script that you know is tested and proven to be effective. And most importantly, pay attention to the people you're speaking with. Have an authentic conversation with them.

First

Be in rapport with yourself.

Remember that a relationship that is in rapport is marked with harmony, accord, affinity. If you want to attract others to that kind of experience with you, you have to have that kind of relationship with yourself first.

Joseph Chilton Pearce, author of *The Crack in the Cosmic Egg*, said that 95% of our communications with people are on an unconscious level. People are going to pick up on whether we're in alignment with our life's mission and are in rapport with who we are. If you're not in rapport with yourself, it's very difficult to have rapport with others.

When you first go into this work, you may not have the confidence you'll soon build with experience, but you can take action now to build your self-esteem and positive outlook on your life and the world. Commit to a new discipline of self-development. Plug into all the books, trainings, and programs that your company provides.

I also advise my clients to go on a negativity fast. For 30 days, try to stay away from negative tv programming, newspapers, even negative people if you can manage it. Surround yourself with people who share your goals ambitions, values, and dreams. Hang out with your team in your network marketing business. You'll never find a more positive group of people. That's what's kept me in this industry for 25 years.

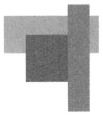

Romi Neustadt

" I still wake up every single morning so excited about my business because I get to have a profound, positive impact on people that I was never able to have when I was a lawyer and PR exec.

I have the privilege of helping people design the lives they really want. When we are able to create larger incomes that provide more time, money, flexibility, and freedom, we're able to pay it forward to our communities and the causes we hold near and dear to our hearts. "

Best

Recognize the value of this business.

Really understand everything that is possible with this business model and the products you are representing. You are limited only by your goals and what you're willing to do to achieve those goals.

With this model, anything is possible. Do you want a little extra money for a shoe fund or a vacation fund? Or maybe you want to replace lost income, if someone in your family has lost a job. Or maybe you want to leave your full-time job. Or maybe you want *transformative income*, where everything can change for you.

Some people are reticent to even accept the potential of being involved in network marketing because they're so used to not dreaming bigger. They're so used to assuming that if something is this good, it has to be too good to be true.

Worst

Believe you don't deserve success.

I work with a lot of professional women who deeply want more time with their families but they don't believe they deserve anything better than the hamster wheel of a conventional corporate job. Success isn't just something that happens to other people. It can happen to anyone, regardless of background, education, finances, or social standing. It all depends on you: Are you coachable? Are

you willing to talk to enough people? And do you believe in yourself?

I'm really passionate about helping people discover
that they do deserve this kind of success and that it's
within their reach.

Give yourself permission to dream bigger than you
ever have before. Surround yourself with people who
agree that success is available to anyone who is willing
to work hard enough for it. Stay away from the naysayers, and give yourself permission to clean house of all
the negative influences in your life. Instead, feed your
head with positive, personal development and fill your
world with positive people.

Unlike other careers where you are paid to be on top of
all situations and business challenges, with network marketing, it's okay to show up not knowing everything. In
fact, you're expected to. Allow yourself to be vulnerable
enough to say, "I need help," and we'll connect you with
someone who will give you the knowledge and support
you need. What a great safety net that is!

This is a business of working for yourself, but not by
yourself. Open yourself up to mentoring relationships.
And you'll find all the support you'll need all around you,
right there for the taking.

First

Remember you're in business.

Decide that you're going to be successful, and that you're
going to run your business like a business, not a hobby. The

vast majority of us start this work in part-time hours, but that doesn't make you any less of the CEO of your own business. Success isn't going to fall from the sky. You have go after it with a business mindset.

This is an incredibly powerful business model through which we get to help motivated people to do extraordinary things. So look for motivated people who see what you see.

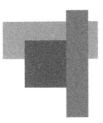

Jeff Olson

" Network marketing brilliantly allows people to become better – not just financially but also as individuals. Their health becomes better, their outlook on life becomes better, their relationships become better.

And when the whole person becomes better, the business works. For me, I'm driven to help people take responsibility for their lives. When they do, they touch other people. And that's what brings true happiness in this world. "

Best

Give yourself time to grow.

It's going to take you at least the first full year just to figure out the business and learn your company's products.
But if you do it right, the person you will become by the
end of that first year will be worth everything you did.

Everything else being equal, the difference between one
person succeeding and the other person failing is the extent to which the successful person is dedicated to their
personal wellness and healthy attitude – or, what I call
your life philosophy. The books you read, the tapes you
listen to, the people you associate with, your personal
health routines, all those things affect your philosophy in
life. A good philosophy turns into a good attitude. And
that turns into success-building actions.

In this business you're a messenger. But not everyone is
a great messenger at first. You might need a year or more
to weed your garden, so to speak, improve your life and
attitude about yourself, and learn more about the business
you're in now. And then, all of a sudden, you will find that
you have become the messenger that other people will want
to listen to. Then watch your business grow.

Worst

Start with unrealistic expectations.

We have the tendency in this business to attract and recruit new people by highlighting the superstars. But that

just ends up giving people unrealistic expectations about what the immediate future is going to look like. You don't want people attracted to get-rich-quick schemes because they'll destroy your company. You want people who are mature, who understand that there's a natural rhythm to being an entrepreneur: You've got to plant seeds, cultivate, and then harvest. And, frankly, that takes time.

If you get into a company as a complete beginner, and you make $10,000 the first month, there's probably something wrong with the opportunity. No legitimate model can perform like that. It's impossible, unless you're making people buy inventory they don't need.

You've got to start slow to grow in a sustainable way. And the company you pick needs to demonstrate its commitment to that philosophy in the way it talks about what's possible in the early phases.

First
Learn how to learn.

People in this business can be divided into two segments: givers and takers. Givers are attractive; they brighten any room they walk into. And your commitment to personal development will give you that energy to be a giver. The first step to learning how to develop yourself personally is to learn how to learn.

In my company we teach people to read at least 10 pages of a good book every day. That's 3,650 pages a year – or roughly 12 books. When those books are the right books – in that they teach you how to positively and efficiently activate your new knowledge – you will massively shift your philosophy by the end of that year.

Reading might feel like it takes a lot of time. But look at it this way: Someone spent their whole life learning something, and then they wrote a book about it. You could spend your life making the same mistakes they made. Or you could just read the book and master the lessons in just two or three days.

But learning doesn't involve just reading. Learning is a two-pronged process: learned knowledge, activity, learn, activity, learn, activity. Each component builds on the other – walking you up the success ladder step by step. Do that long enough and then all of a sudden people will look to you as a role model. As soon as you become worthy of that, you become the teacher. And as soon as you become the teacher, that's when your business grows.

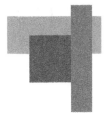

Ken Porter

" As network marketers, we are ambassadors of good. We all want to spread love, and we want our fellow man to enjoy what we have. I don't know any other profession where sharing these gifts is embedded in leaders' motivations.

This business makes me cry all the time. I'm so grateful that I can be blessed enough to be a part of it and have a lifetime of making other people's lives better. "

Best

Believe that you will succeed.

Your success in this business model has everything to do with who you are at your most fundamental level – what I call your programmed DNA. If you have a history of starting something, quitting, and failing over and over again, you're going to fail here, too. Somewhere in your early life you taught yourself that quitting is acceptable.

If you have trained yourself incorrectly throughout your lifetime, you can break that pattern and start afresh today. Get rid of excuses. Take responsibility. Don't accept the belief that it's the company's fault, your upline's fault, your side line's fault, the comp plan's fault, or the product's fault. All that baloney goes right out the window. It all comes directly back to you.

If you are going to be successful, you have to take ownership of your commitment to succeed. And you don't quit. Ever. Successful people succeed because they have trained their DNA to finish what they start. It's what they do.

Worst

Use advertising and cold-calling.

I want you to gain your confidence and make your mistakes with people who are close to you, as opposed to strangers. I want you talking with your mom. I want you practicing with your sister. I want you to develop the skill set you need right there close to your home where it's safe.

Don't try to take the networking out of network marketing. All success starts close to home. From there you can cover the world. My gigantic Japanese team comes from people near my home in Monroe, UT. My contacts for India came from someone who is only two degrees away from my personal list. I've been at this over 20 years, and I'm still working through my list of warm contacts.

All the money is in prospecting. That's what all the people who make money do – it doesn't matter what business they're in. That means you're a prospector too. It just happens that of all the compensation plans created for prospectors, our industry has the best one. It's the only compensation plan that multiplies on itself.

First

Embrace this business as your future.

All of us pursue our most compelling desires. People are always telling me about their dreams. But then I say to them, "Your mouth says this, but the real proof of your desires is born out of your pursuits. So no matter what you say, if you're pursuing the football games and television, well, that's your real desire."

Unless you're fully committed to network marketing and what it offers you in terms of future rewards, it's just a wish. Not a dream. A mere wish.

When I took on this business, I took my hobbies, my other goals and dreams and even my job, and I consolidated them into this singular goal of succeeding in network marketing. I no longer wanted a promotion in my job; I no longer wanted a raise; I no longer expected that I would be there in three years. I had to have a job, but the truth is that I went through four different jobs while building my network. They were all junk jobs. I had to earn an income but my network was my singular focus.

All my future was wrapped up in network marketing. I pinned everything in my life on that singular thing that was going to take me where I wanted to go. So everything else became second, third, and fourth place.

Most people can't see past their current pain today. So they make all their decisions based on this moment in time. And they make all the wrong decisions. So people subordinate their dreams all the time to whatever brings them the least amount of pain today. But you can't subordinate your dreams to the last amount of pain and ever expect to achieve them. Your dreams must be preeminent.

Jules Price

" The beauty about network marketing is that the major focus gets to be on the people you root for; not on yourself. You feel an immeasurable sense of fulfillment from helping other people get what they want. It's been such an amazing shift in my life, from trying to be the best "me," to then also turning my energies to include the notion of, "How many people can I help?" "

Best

Tell stories from the heart.

Have you ever been to a movie that pulls you in so emotionally that you suddenly start to cry at an especially powerful scene? That's because you've completely identified with the character. The same thing happens when you powerfully share your story about the first time you discovered the product or joined the business. Your prospects are so caught up with your tale that they follow along, imagining themselves in that situation.

Telling stories is a much more effective approach than merely sharing a typical business presentation of data and facts. It's a very powerful vehicle to help your prospects envision themselves being part of what you offer. While they're listening, they're asking themselves, "Would I want to work with this person? Is this endeavor going to be fun? Am I going to be in a better place than I am now by doing it? Do I want to give up my TV at night to work on this business?"

People base their decisions largely on instinct and what they're feeling. If it feels good to them on a deep, emotional level, that will be the influence that guides their decision.

Worst

Lose your perspective.

People begin their business with high hopes and expectations. They see network marketing as the highway to helping themselves and others achieve their dreams. But they risk getting blindsided by even the smallest disappointment or bad day. Why? They've lost their perspective somewhere along the way.

Perspective is defined as a sensible way of judging how good, bad, or important one thing is as compared with other things. So when the bad becomes so bad that it overwhelms the perceived potential of the good, or when your obstacles become much bigger than your dreams, you need to readjust your perspective.

Dreams can also seem impossibly far away when you lose perspective. In the art world, perspective is achieved by making far-away objects smaller. When your perspective in network marketing is skewed by inevitable challenges and disappointments, the vision of your dreams can appear so small that it seems too far away to ever attain. But really, it's all in how you discipline yourself to evaluate your situation.

Keeping a healthy sense of humor will always help you hold onto the proper perspective in any business. It helps you to continually reevaluate remember what's truly important. Being able to see the lighter side of a situation can protect you and help you get back up again when you're blindsided by unexpected circumstances or major obstacles that arise.

First

Commit to authentic relationships.

Relationships are the fundamental building blocks that anchor your ability to succeed in business. When you grow and maintain great relationships with others and keep your focus on being a connector of people, you will be amazed how much this value comes back to you tenfold.

If you're building authentic relationships as you sort through the world looking for those who are meant to come into your business, you're treating people like people, rather than like prospects. If someone doesn't want to be a customer or distributor, keep in touch with them anyway. Call them now and then just to say, "Hi." Send them little things that let them know you're thinking about them. Look for ways to do special, small gestures to make people say, "Wow! I can't believe you thought of me." I live by the phrase, "Go the extra mile. It's never crowded."

Paula Pritchard

" I love network marketing because of how it changes lives. When I first became involved I was motivated by financial goals, and that drove me to be successful. But once I achieved those goals, I realized that there was something bigger that network marketing offered – freedom.

To be financially free is like nothing else. Just when I thought I had the ultimate, I was able to help someone else become a millionaire. That was when I thought, 'Oh my gosh, this is the ultimate of the ultimate.' "

Best

Use your resources strategically.

Remember that whoever recruits the most frontline people wins. In the first 90 days of your business, you should be spending 80% building your front line, and the remaining 20% doing three-way calls for your downline. Don't look to the left, don't look to the right. For those first 90 days, recruit like a crazy person. Get the right number of people into your organization initially.

In my particular case, I know that if I have six to seven people on each team, my group will be a success. So remember the laws of averages as you're recruiting your initial group of people. For every three people I talk to, one will want to see the business. For every three people who see the business, one will get in. For every three people who want to get in, one will do something with the business.

After your first 90 days of filling your frontline with people, flip your energies to focus 80% of your time and energy on building your downline. Only 20% should be focused on your frontline.

Worst

Give your energy to non-performers.

One of the mistakes that everyone makes is to work hard with people who end up never making their sponsor a dime. These people talk the talk but don't walk the walk. And you must block out what they're saying and start watching what they do.

If they're doing what you're doing, if they are a clone of you; if they're coming out of the gate as a self-starter; doing exactly what you told them to do; then you start paying attention to these people. If you don't, you're taking away your energies from the people who really can make it happen for you and who deserve your support.

You can't want success for them more than they want it themselves. You have to stay emotionally detached from everyone until they start demonstrating that they will be with you, working hard for the long haul. Otherwise it's too heartbreaking and painful when they leave.

First

Be clear about your teams' *whys.*

Knowing your team members' *whys* is a double-sided motivational tool. If you know your team member dreams of travel, you can send him a postcard of the Amalfi Coast when you go on your own trip. If another team member wants a Jaguar convertible, send her pictures of one, to let her know you're thinking of her.

Your team members will be so honored that you are so committed and aware of their specific dreams.

On the other hand, knowing what your team members' *whys* are gives you a tool to remind them when they are losing their focus and dedication to growing their business. Knowing their dreams gives you meaningful leverage. This is when you sit down with them, remind them specifically of their dream and then say, "I'm doing what I need to do to help you be successful. But at every turn you've got a roadblock. I need to apologize to you for pushing you too hard. Do we need to reassess?"

Being able to speak specifically of their dreams gives you a valuable tool to reinspire them.

Bob Quintana

" Every time I shake someone's hand; every time I turn a door knob and walk into the next meeting; every time I pick up the phone and speak with that next person, this could be the next ace in my business; or the person who leads me to the next ace. Who knows when that serious player will appear? Maybe a day or two down the road. Or a year or two down the road. That's part of the fun. That's part of the excitement. "

Best

Make recruiting a game. Keep it fun.

People put too much pressure on themselves to perform. They want to recruit top performers immediately. But running a business in network marketing is a lot like flipping a well-shuffled deck (or multiple decks) of cards. Every time we introduce our opportunity to a new person, we're flipping another card, looking for the aces. We know they're in there somewhere. We just don't know where they are. We might get lucky and turn over an ace or two right away. Or they might be in the middle of the deck, and we'll have to flip 15, 20, or 25 cards. Or they may even be at the bottom of the deck, with 35, 45, or more, flips required before we come up with that first ace. We never know who that next "flip of the card" will end up becoming, or leading us to. So we need to make it fun.

Here's what you can be sure of: If we flip enough cards, we're going to find the aces. If we focus on the excitement of the possibility of an ace showing up with the next flip, it can (and should) be really enjoyable. So let's all just fall in love with the process of *flipping cards*. Let's show our opportunity to as many people as necessary to find our aces – and let's have fun doing it!

Worst

Lose your sense of detachment.

Let's say you find a potential ace, who has what it takes to win big in your business. But that person still says *no*.

This has happened to every successful network marketer. While this can be frustrating, the key to handling it effectively is to remain *detached* from your candidate's ultimate decision to get involved with you. Keep in mind that there is most likely something else going on in that person's life that is preventing him or her from seeing that your opportunity is right. Don't take it personally. It's most likely not about you. Remember that we can't really know what's going on in people's lives behind the scenes – often not even our best friends or family.

When people say *no* and you take it personally, you become attached to the outcome rather than detached, and you take the fun out of building your organization. All we can control is showing our opportunity using our company's proven methods, then let the chips fall where they may. If it's the 'right time' for your prospects, they'll get in. If it's not, they won't. And remember, a *no* today can be a *yes* at some point down the road.

Just stay detached and keep showing your opportunity. You'll find the people you're looking for.

First

Commit to personal development.

Personal development is a key component that keeps people committed to the business over time. Reading empowering books; listening to great CDs; attending trainings with top leaders; going to other live seminars that support your growth are all a part of this. Here's the coolest thing: personal development begins with *one*…reading *one* book; listening to *one* CD; attending *one* training…

and then the next *one*! Don't let the task of self-improvement overwhelm you. Just take it one step at a time.

Ongoing personal development for yourself and your team will dramatically accelerate the growth of your networking business. So, make sure it's not only part of your own personal commitment, but that it's also part of your organization's. I regularly recommend (and often give out) specific books and CDs that I've found valuable.

Establishing the habit of ongoing personal and professional development will help you and your team develop the proper mindset, the skillset, and level of execution necessary to win big in network marketing, and in life! So, begin with *one*... and begin now!

Jeremy Reynolds

" Business people do better in network marketing than most because they understand business. They understand revenue-producing activities versus time wasters. They understand it's all about productivity. They understand that you're only really selling when you're showing up. "

Best

Recruit corporate executives.

Business people are equipped to do really well in network marketing because they come into it already understanding the fundamentals of the ways an enterprise becomes profitable. They understand revenue-producing activities versus those tasks and projects that are time-wasters. They understand that they're only really selling when they're out there showing the business to people. They understand that making a difference in the world depends on doing it in partnership with others. They can't do that just sitting behind a desk and waiting for the phone to ring. They get that.

But, even so, we have to remember that our business is not for everyone in the corporate world. If you are satisfied with your leather briefcase, your room full of smart corporate people and all of those things that come with a corporate job, God bless you. I'm so happy for you that you've found contentment and fulfillment.

But I will ask you, "Do you want something more? If you're looking, I'm looking for people who are looking for something more. But if it's not for you, maybe you know someone who is not as happy as you are."

Worst

Rush the process.

People who are already sophisticated business people require a lot more time invested in discovering common ground before you dive into introducing your opportunity. So what I typically do with these individuals is go into storytelling mode so they know that I've worked my way up the corporate ladder, too. And that it was just leaning on the wrong wall, as Stephen Covey said.

I tell them I wasn't happy in the corporate world. And that there was always something impeding my progress because the next level I was striving for was already occupied by a VP or a senior VP. And that the only way I could advance would be if that person left the company or died. I didn't like the politics. So I found a better way.

Only then would I talk about how with network marketing a person can reclaim his or her time, own the results of their efforts, and build equity in their own business, etc.

First

Find the need and then fill it.

Our business is about building relationships. You have to take the time to understand people and make sure they understand who you are. And then together you can find a solution to whatever is challenging them. Then you'll know whether to lead with the product or the opportunity.

I usually do my relationship building in two steps. The first is to make the contact to find out what is going on with that person. The second is to come back to them a little later and say, "Hey, I've identified a solution to that thing we were talking about. I've been thinking a lot about you, can we sit down again so that I can share this idea with you?"

The questions are a little different when you're talking with a corporate executive or professional. I will ask, "Tell me about your experience. Tell me what you love about your job. What does your five-year plan look like? Do you have the ability to freely advance in your organization? Or are you like I was? Because if you are where I was, I'm here to partner with you and we can have some fun building something that is all yours."

I have this exact conversation with business people all the time. They want to know the answer to the same question: "Show me how I make money." They want to know how to leverage their resources, how to get a return on their investment. Those are the questions a businessperson asks.

Matthew Riddell

" Remember to share what you've learned with your team. People need to see you be real and vulnerable. You should never get to the point where you're in an ivory tower and untouchable. Always look for ways to get outside your comfort zone. That's one way to set a good example. "

Best

See obstacles as a chance to grow.

When you frame them right in your mind, they're easier to deal with. Think of them as stepping stones. Roadblocks will ultimately benefit you and improve your skills as a business leader. They're not there to hurt you. They're there to teach you.

And there is always a way through them. Ask yourself if there is someone at a higher level in the company who can help you? The answer is always *yes*. Do not try to go around these roadblocks alone. Your sponsor and support team have been there before and can see what's happening more clearly than you can.

And when they tell you what to do, don't procrastinate taking action by asking another 25,000 questions. Just do it. The answers will come in the actions you take. Do it, and then talk about it with your team.

Likewise, welcome plateaus, as frustrating as they are. You're mastering network marketing, and the mastery path is never a journey straight up the mountain. There are plateaus along the way that force you to pause and wait for the next spurt of progress. You're going to get bored doing the same thing over and over again with no visible sign of results.

But in fact, you're actually getting better at the skills required for your new level. So enjoy the plateaus, because that's where you're truly acquiring mastery and allowing your new skills to integrate into your subconscious.

Plateaus are where you practice, practice, practice, making your new role as a leader second nature to you. So welcome them.

Worst

Make money your main motivator.

Don't just purely chase the dollars. Success eludes people who are just in it for the money. People who are just focused on the bottom line miss the beauty of the profession, which is being of service to others. Focus on that, and the rest takes care of itself.

This profession isn't about pressure, it's about service. Not everyone will see what you see, exactly when you see it. Love people where they are. Be patient with them and be a good example. And be ready to help them when the timing is right. If you talk with 100 people, 30 of them will likely be open to have a chat. The other 70 may have a lot going on. If you pressure, they'll run away. That's a common experience that gives the industry a bad name.

First

Do your homework on the profession.

As you learn about it, you'll come to the overwhelming realization that network marketing is still in its infancy. It has all the win/win/win benefits. It's a win for the company because it has a whole group of people who are evangelical about their products, eager to share what they love with others. The customers get the best service you can imagine. And the people building their teams have a wonderful business with little to no overhead. And they can work from home.

The corporate world is a dinosaur model. If you get into the corporate world, the company's number one interest is in keeping you stuck in a job that you're good at. But in network marketing, our number one interest is in making you better at what you do, because that's how all the money gets made. There's a direct link between productivity and payment.

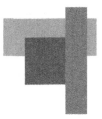

Sarah Robbins

" We were recently on a rewards trip to Italy. At the end of one of the days, we were on a bus going from a winery back to the hotel. I sat in the back, alone with my thoughts. People might have thought there was something wrong, I was so quiet.

But I was just looking at all these leaders and thinking about how we have all changed each others' lives. This is what it's all about. Not the product. It's the people. And our amazing transformation as a team. "

Best

Love working with people.

What do all the top leaders in network marketing have in common? It might not be so easy to tell at first glance. I'm a former kindergarten teacher. My company also has a former attorney, a make-up artist, lots of stay-at-home moms, and even a figure skater. What do we have in common? Other than having big hearts and big dreams, we love working with people.

This is not a product business, it's about helping people build their dreams. When you understand this and keep that distinction top of mind, everything you do will be determined by your primary drive of bringing success to others.

Most importantly, you'll be developing a culture of recognition and praise. People work harder for praises than they will raises. So celebrate the little successes with as much enthusiasm as you will the big leaps of growth.

Celebrate your new team member's first customer or first new enrollee. Mark the occasion of their first solo presentation with a small gift. They don't have to be elaborate. A small gift card from their favorite store works wonders.

Worst

Let discouragement take over.

There are times when your prospects will turn you down. There are times when your friends and family won't "get" what you're doing. There are times when team members will quit. There may even be times where you encounter conflict occurring on your team, and find yourself disappointed. As leaders we have to learn how to handle these events in such a way that benefits the whole team – starting with role modeling our own behavior.

We all have a choice to remain rooted and grounded in the way we respond to disappointments and frustrations. When we get that text or email that starts our day off wrong, or when we get that call that upsets us, we have a choice to react or respond.

Reaction is an emotional decision often commanded by our emotions or exhaustion. Response is a thought-out reply, setting emotions aside, leading with logic, love, and leadership resolutions.

How we treat people can have a great impact on the degree to which we progress in our business. The main thing is to remember that when there's conflict, there's usually a lack of communication. As the leader it's your job to listen. Don't respond or defend. Don't make it about you. Make it about your wonderful team and the collaborative spirit you are nurturing.

First

Know your team members' *whys.*

People will tell you to be clear about what your *why*. Which is true. But when you want to build a vibrant team of people working together and support each other toward their goals, you have to know what those goals are.

In a truly collaborative team, not only do the sponsors know their team members' *why*, but team members themselves know what each others' motivations and passions are. This way they can talk to each other and support each other in ways that are particularly meaningful. This way they can help each other discipline their disappointments and stay on track toward their individual goals.

We can also help each other grow new goals and dreams as we hit our current objectives and seek out even bigger *whys*. When I started, I was a kindergarten teacher, in a bad economy in a troubled part of the country. I could see the writing on the wall about my own job prospects and was looking for a back-up plan for financial stability. Now I'm dreaming about using my income to establish and support a foundation for disadvantaged children.

These are dreams that are possible in a culture of collaboration among leaders who deeply and authentically care about each other.

Teresa Romain

" Debt is a claim on your future income. And since we spend time and energy making money, debt is also a claim on your future time and energy. Don't start your business by creating a burden on your future income, time, and energy. Instead, run your business in a way that you're creating more freedom in the future. If you get that freedom and still make a gazillion dollars, woo! Bonus! How wonderful is that? "

Best

Pay off debt with your first profits.

Use the first money that you make to rapidly pay off your debt. You can experience financial freedom in this business even if you never make lots of money. Most people who go into this business have debt. So don't be ashamed if you're among them.

Remember, though, without debt you have many more options in your life. You can quit that job that you don't like and do something you love much sooner. You can be mortgage-free in as little as six to eight years. It's amazing what just an extra $200 to $400 a month can do to change your life for the better. And that's so doable.

When you're debt-free, your life changes. Take that initial early profit to pay off your debt and then you'll be free to make lots of money in this business, if you want to.

Worst

Go into debt trying to make money.

There's a gambling expression, "To bet on the come." It means that you borrow money on the expectation that the next hand will give you the big win that will make you rich. The thought is, "It's okay to spend all this money now because one day I'll make oodles of money and then I'll pay off my debt." By doing that, you create an experience of pressure, fear, and attachment to the result.

The worst thing you can do is fund your business with debt. You find yourself thinking, "It's okay that I'm charging this expense, because I'll be making more money in the future. And everything will be taken care of." But making more money doesn't necessarily mean you're financially free. It could mean that you're making more money to service a bigger debt. And you will never get out from under with that kind of thinking.

True, as the saying goes, "You need to crack three eggs to make an omelet." Which means that you have to spend money to make money. But you don't need to crack open 30 eggs.

From the very beginning, think of this business as a part-time enterprise that pays for itself.

First

Open a separate bank account.

Determine how much money you can afford to start your business with little or no risk. Put that money in a dedicated business checking account. And make that checking account pay for your business. And pay yourself from that account.

This way you'll have to think about what you're spending that money on in your business. It's going to force you to think about profit from the very beginning, as well as focus on what actions make money now, not one day in the future.

When you pay yourself directly from the business account, you'll quickly see when you start to make money. It just makes everything so clear.

A separate bank account supports a structure and a discipline to your thinking. You can quickly see when you make money if the sum isn't comingled with other income sources. You can more quickly identify which actions are profit generators, and which waste your time. You are less likely to go into a debt spiral when you have a separate bank account that's just for your business only, and when you make your business pay for its expenses. If, for instance, you only have $500 to start your business with, you will be less likely (and you really shouldn't) draw $1,500 from your other financial resources to pay for a starter kit.

Do what you can with the money that you have assigned to the business, and make your profit with that. And then, with that profit, you can increase to the next level.

Hilde & Orjan Saele

"   **Orjan:** Network marketing is much like race car driving. You have all the systems backing you up: the high-performance car, all its components and a world class pit crew. You put in your skill, practice time, and courage. And you're the one who gets the check, the praises, and prizes when you win.

Hilde: Success is not about the system in itself, it is all about who you are and how you work the business. Remember that the key to win is to build strong relationships with your team. **"**

Best

H: Understand the system's power.

It's important to understand why you need a system as soon as possible. The system will save you time, stress, and, in the end, money. The good network marketing companies have set up systems to help you get new customers and distributors, and keep them on your team. Just as the system will guide and develop you, you will be able to count on it do to the same for your distributors so they too will know exactly what to do.

The system will give you clarity and certainty. Knowing exactly what to do, how to do it, and what kinds of expectations you can have -- that's what creates motivation and will keep people on your team for the long run.

O: Be hungry, hone-able, honorable

In their book, *Launching a Leadership Revolution*, Chris Brady and Orrin Woodward talk about the three H's that are essential to becoming a great leader. Being hungry makes you committed to investing the work and time necessary to be successful. Being hone-able means being willing to be coached and developed in the way that will make you most likely to succeed in network marketing.

Finally, being honorable requires you to keep your word, be honest, and be the person your team can always depend on to carry through on your commitments and support of their efforts and dreams. Network marketing is about trust. And trust must start with you.

Worst

O: Don't train on the system.

Knowing the system itself is not enough. You have to take the time to train on all the steps that go into implementing the system. For instance, you've got to "make a list of your warm market" as a part of your system. Now you have to actually train on what goes behind that list. Who do you put on that list? How exactly do you invite these people to a meeting? We actually have a five-step system behind the invitation step alone.

H: Be bossy.

As much as you have faith in your company's system, and as committed you are to training it, there will be people who want to try other techniques and approaches. You can't just tell them, "No, you're not allowed to." Remember, the people in your team are entrepreneurial and they have an independent streak. So you can't just tell them no. You'll drive them away.

You can advise them though. You can point out stories from past experience where a similar approach was tried, and it didn't work.

First

H: Activate your system right away.

When a new distributor gets started, the first thing we do is put them through the "getting started" training, which includes some product training. Then we have

them create a list of 100 names of their contacts to identify 10 potential customers and 10 potential distributors.
Third: We start goal setting. Fourth: We teach product
demonstrations and business presentations. At the same
time, we start reaching out to their prospects and invite
them to meetings.

O: Focus on what duplicates.

We have a saying in network marketing, "It's not what
works, it's what duplicates." This is why it's essential to
embrace *systems thinking* from the very beginning. There
are many innovative things we as individuals can do to
create new customers and distributors. The question is:
Will they duplicate in the second, third, or fourth levels
of your organization? That's where you may not have
direct influence on your distributors' conversation with
their own prospects.

Think of it this way: You may want to create a beautiful, hand-crafted work of art. But you won't be able to
distribute it to every home in your country. If you want
every home to have your work, you have to have it ma-
chine crafted. Otherwise it will never get into the hands of
people who need or want it.

Tim Sales

" In network marketing, the power is in the people. Companies don't build. Products don't build. People are the ones who build. And in this profession you are given the tools and training to build something wonderful for you and the people you care about. With so much else going on in the world today, this is the profession in which you can declare and live out your faith and confidence in people. "

Best

Fall in love with your new profession.

To be successful in network marketing, you're going to have to fall in love with some aspect of the business. There has to be something that fires you up so that you can deliver a compelling presentation to the people you speak with. This passion is what will keep you engaged even in those times when you wonder whether all this hard work is worth it. It is the passion for the work that will give you the resilience you need to stick with it, even during the painful times. Just like with any love story, it is the challenging times that will strengthen the relationship you have with your business and your organization.

It is the love that you have for the business that will drive you to invest your passion, your time, and your self-development so that you get better at network marketing.

It doesn't even have to be the story of how the product has improved your own life that fires you up. It can be what that product does for other people. I met a military vet once who told me, "Tim, I'm at 6% body fat. I can't get personally excited about the diet product in my company." Then he went to a convention and met a woman who lost 120 pounds in five months by using the shake. She still had over 300 pounds to lose, but everyone in the room fell in love with both the product and her. They could see how the company had offered her a pathway to health that seemed so far beyond her grasp. My friend came home and said, "Tim I get it." And now he's unstoppable.

Worst

Be unprepared for objections.

There are so many different variations on the theme of why network marketing is a bad business model. "That's not one of those pyramid schemes, is it?" "Oh, it's not like that company, is it?" "My friends signed on 30 years ago and wouldn't leave me alone until I went to one of those dumb meetings with the circles. We're no longer friends." "I tried one of those businesses and it didn't work."

Each time someone says something like that to you, it's going to feel like a punch in the nose. But these objections are predictable. You absolutely can learn the right responses to each one of those. Get educated before you get out there.

First

Know your company.

The beauty of network marketing is that you get to learn your new profession while you actually begin practicing. Still, it's overwhelming at first because it's hard to know where to start your learning process. So here's my advice:

Learn everything you can about the company. Learn all about the products. Don't just focus on the product line itself. Learn what differentiates them from the competitors' products. For instance, vitamins are vitamins. You can get them from the drug store, from the supermarket, from the health food store, or from your company.

Exactly why should your customers get them from you over all the other choices out there?

Learn about your company's leadership. Who's your CEO and what's his or her background? What is it about your company's executives that make them a good team to sign on with? You may think that your team is your sponsor, your upline, and the organization you will build. But you're also a member of the corporate team and they are just as important for you to identify with and respect as anyone you will work with more directly.

Tom "Big Al" Schreiter

" I love network marketing because you can associate with people who are negative and who have given up on their dreams. Or, you can associate with network marketers who are positive, forward-thinking, people with dreams. Guess which group would be more fun to take a cruise with. "

Best

Do things in the right order.

1. **Build rapport based on trust.** If people don't trust you, you are out of luck. Even if you have the best product or service in the world, you're toast if people don't trust you. The way to build instant and immediate rapport is to tell someone a fact that they already know to be true. They will think you are a genius; that you see the world from the same view point. Pick a statement that everyone will agree with. For example: "Jobs interfere with our week, wouldn't you say?" Or, "Commuting is really, really hard," or, "We would all like to look younger, right?"

Ask the right questions. You can start a conversation with even the coldest, most introverted person out there. You may have nothing in common, but if you use these four words, you can get them talking: "I am just curious…" For example: "I am just curious, do you enjoy working hard so your boss has a big house for his retirement?"

2. **Break the ice.** This is where we introduce our business into a social conversation. There are certain words that grab their attention: "I just found out…." The survival mechanism in every person stops cold, because they want to know what you found out and if it's relevant to them. Some examples are: "I just found out how we can get an extra paycheck every month." Or, "I just found out how we can fire our boss," or, "I just found out how we can make more money part time than our

spouses do full-time." The next words out of your prospect's mouth will be "How?"

3. **Close.** The close comes before the presentation. We are going to close the prospect first, have them make a decision, so really the presentation will be their first training session. People decide things in an instant, long before they have all the information. That is why it is important not to use random untrained words. To close your prospect, use these words, "Would it be okay...." Here are some examples: "Would it be okay if you got an extra paycheck every month?" "Would it be okay if your skin got younger while you were asleep?" "Would it be okay if you never had to commute again?"

4. **Make the presentation.** Use your company's tools.

Worst

Use random, untrained words

Early in my career I found lots of great prospects, and proceeded to ruin them with my "untrained" words. I thought success was finding the right person. Success in prospecting is not in finding the right person, but in saying the right words to anyone we are communicating with. Almost everyone is pre-sold on our business. They would love to have our product or service in their lives, and they would love to have more money in their lives. All we have to do is avoid using "untrained" words that talk them out of it.

I sometimes joke with distributors who sell nutritional products. I ask them, "Do your prospects want to live longer? Or die quickly?" They answer, "Live longer." And then I ask, "Do your prospects want more money or less?" They answer, "More money." And then I ask, "So if your prospects want to live longer, and you offer them a chance to ... and they want more money, and you offer them that as well ... what do they say when you finish your presentation?" The distributors answer, "No."

So what has happened? They have taken a pre-sold prospect and "talked them out of it" with their random, "untrained" words.

First

Practice trained words.

In contrast, "trained words" will open people's minds, and have them begging for your presentation. They will have said *yes* before you have said a word about your company, product, or service. Role play and practice these 13 words: I am just curious...; I just found out...; Would it be okay if....

Here is how they might sound all together. " I am just curious, how many people here would like to feel a lot younger? Well, I just found out how we can do that. Would it be okay if you tried it for a month and see what it does for you?"

Jerry Scribner

" Network marketing can have an incredible impact on our economy in terms of helping families get out of debt. We're being buried by credit card and student loan debt. If we can turn that around through network marketing, that's better than achieving a pin level. "

Best

Make personal growth top priority.

People who blossom in network marketing become better people. Just making money will make you more of what you already are. If you're a good person before you start making money, you'll be an even better person. When I first started in network marketing, I gravitated to people who were continually on the path to personal development and success. That doesn't mean they don't have bad times and issues in their life, but they're focused on personal growth.

When I joined network marketing, I was a negative person. I had given up on life in terms of trying to get ahead. I had settled in. I had a roof over my head. I wasn't missing any meals. I had a car. It could have been a whole lot worse. But that mentality was absolutely going to stop me from having the success I wanted in network marketing. I had to start dreaming again. The first thing that my wife and I dreamed about was getting our two daughters through college. That was the entire reason we got involved. To make $400 to $500 per month to get those two girls through college. Since then it's become much, much more.

Worst

Overwhelm yourself.

In the beginning, people don't have the strong belief in the potential of the business. So it's difficult for them to say, "I'm going to go out and take care of kids in Africa," or some other big vision. That will come soon enough.

Most people aren't going to have a big *why* in the beginning. They're looking at this business wondering if it's even going to work for them. So I'm just going to incrementally bring them along the way and help them achieve little goals along the way so their belief levels go up.

I like to find something that's very attainable for them to achieve in the first couple of weeks or months as small *whys*. And we gradually build their belief factor for whatever their *why* is in the long run.

The more their belief level goes up and they marry it with personal development, the more likely they'll be to achieve anything they want.

First

Find a great mentor.

I'd love for my new team members to read personal development books, listen to CDs, and go to seminars. But they need to take it one step at a time. They need baby's milk, not meat. So in the beginning I may give them a short book to read to get them started. They'll see that I can be their mentor. But, ultimately, they're going to be seeking different people along the way to connect with them.

We have four different pin levels in our company. And when someone joins, I give them the contact information of a person at each of the pin levels, and I encourage them to call them and introduce themselves with these words:

"I'm brand new and I understand that you're in my sponsorship line. I'd appreciate any help you can give me."

Get those relationships going.

I also tell new people, "Put yourself out there. Let yourself be seen. Let people know who you are. Do anything you need to do to feel a part of this team and culture."

They need to get in front of as many people as they possibly can. They need to sit in the front rows at events. They can even ask if they can come along after the event if the speakers and leaders are meeting for dinner. They'll be surprised how often they'll be welcome to sit in.

Bill Silvester

" When I first started out in network marketing, I thought my goal was to get rich. My main question was, "How much money can I make out of this?" But this business started getting really fun and rewarding when I changed my focus to, "How many people can I help make money?"

Now my goal is to help hundreds of Australians and people around the world achieve their goals and dreams. That makes network marketing beautiful. "

Best

Build rapport with questions.

Experienced, successful network marketers will tell you, "Don't firehose prospects with a lot of information all at once." It's hard not to do that when you're excited about the business opportunity and you want people to see its potential. Still we all know what it's like to be talked *at*, not *to*. Here's how you can rein in your excitement and engage your prospect more effectively: Ask questions.

There are six open-end questions that will not only help you avoid overwhelming your prospects but also give you the insights you need to be more effective with each recruit: Who? What? Where? When? Why? And How?

Sincerely ask questions about them; listen carefully – don't just wait until their lips have stopped moving. Give them all the time they need to fully answer. And you will have a wealth of information you need to either match them up with a great product or your business opportunity.

Worst

Ignore the products themselves.

If you don't spend time learning about your company's products and what they can do for you and your customers, you are ignoring a powerful business-building tool.

First of all, you need customers, in addition to building your organization. And secondly, those prospects who could eventually be interested in joining your business might say *no* to the opportunity. But if you tell them about a particular product that will provide a solution they're looking for, you give them another opportunity to experience the company.

First you have to learn about, experience, and use the products yourself. It's not much good if you tell someone that they'll make a lot of money in some vague sense without being able to tell them your first-hand experience with the product that they'll be selling themselves. People want to believe in the products they will be representing to their own friends and customers. You must know the products very well yourself. That's the only way you can invite your prospects to try the products and build their own story.

First

Prepare to be a pioneer.

If you want something that you never had before, you'll have to do what you've never done before. So you'll be pioneering new skills, habits, and disciplines when you take up network marketing.

The first step to being a pioneer is knowing where you're starting from. It's important to know where you want to go, but it's also important to know where you are right now. You know what kind of house you want for your family, in precisely the neighborhood you have identified as safe and beautiful. So where are you living now? What's your living situation like?

Are you currently spending enough time with your children? What kinds of hours are you working now? What kinds of schools are your children going to now? Are you happy with the way they're learning?

Naturally, it's inspiring to know what kind of car you're dreaming about. But what kind of car do you have now?

Know those things and you will have a strong idea of how big the gap is between what your life is like now and what you dream of.

Once you have clearly envisioned the future you want, your goal plan makes more sense. And you will have the resolve to do all the learning, growing, and adventuring you need to do to achieve your dreams. And you'll have the courage to pioneer your new life as you grow into it, leaving your old self behind.

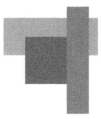

Sean Smith

" You have to make a choice. Whatever that choice is, that's cool. Just understand what the ramifications of that choice are. If you're going to be more committed to your comfort zone, your self-doubts, the old stories from your past, you'll have to check your dreams at the door. Your success lives beyond the walls of your comfort zone. "

Best

Create a space for your business.

Everyone is incredibly busy nowadays. And even the people who aren't busy believe they're busy. People get really excited about the possibilities of network marketing and they see the vision. But they frequently forget to take things off their "plate" so they can add the activities around network marketing to their life.

One of the pitches in the network marketing area is that you can start this business in just a few hours a day or a week. But the question is: Which hours will they be? Get specific and ask yourself, "If I'm going to fit five hours toward my dream, what am I going to trade in?"

Notice I say trade in, not sacrifice. What will you trade in? TV? That's the first place I'd look. Email habits? Most of us spend twice as much time on email than we need to. However you choose to spend your time, just know that you will have to move something off your plate in order to put your dreams onto it.

Worst

Set your heart on specific people.

People who are new to the business get emotionally attached to certain people joining their business. They're so emotionally excited when they first join, they take that excitement and firehose their friends and family. And then it feels like a big personal defeat when those people say *no.* When I first joined a company I called my best friends from high school and proceeded to have a 2.5-hour argument over the business.

With my friends and family, I came across as saying, "You're in or we're not friends." I so wish I hadn't done that. The worst way to begin this business is with a lot of emotional failure, debates, and irritation. That's not how you want to start a business that you're going to make your dreams come true with.

First

Emotionally commit to your vision.

When you're first starting out in network marketing, you're going to feel the excitement and pressure of getting a string of *yeses*. As a result, every interaction is looked at as a win or loss. But it's important to bear in mind that in sales of any kind there are going to be more losses, if win/loss is defined by whether you get a new customer or recruit. Let's face it, the road to success is never a smoothly paved road, it's full of pot holes. If you're not emotionally bought into the bigger picture, it will be easier for you to quit when you run into obstacles.

Your vision for the future is much bigger than the obstacles. So we have to create that emotional buy-in so that you are prepared to go through what you have to go through.

Most people try to get to those goals through will power. But you need to keep your vision alive through a deep, emotional experience that's available by tapping into your *why* power. The way to get that is to go into the future in your imagination and deeply experience what life is like with emotional, time, and financial freedom. Imagine in granular detail what this freedom will be like, using all your senses. It's about programming that future experience into your mind and body now.

When you fully experience the future in this way, you'll be foaming at the mouth to realize that future. You'll be willing to crawl across shards of glass to experience in reality the future you have already experienced emotionally.

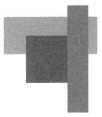

Roman Sobolevsky

" I feel this business as if it were music. This is the symphony, and I am the conductor. And the people in my organization are like musicians in the orchestra with me. If we share this vision, and play this music together, doing it honestly and sincerely, our happiness grows. My wife, Tatiana, and I are able to see how many people have changed their destinies in just two or three years. These people's happiness is our happiness. **"**

Best

Commit to being coachable.

When I enroll someone new, I want to see if that person is ready to follow my advice. My main interest at this point is whether I will be able to count on them as my active business partners. So I want to see new enrollees listen to me, read the books that I have assigned to them, follow my advice, and keep their appointments with me.

During the first month they're in the business, I don't want them talking to anyone about joining the organization. I want to see them investing their time in learning about the network marketing business model, learning about our company, and learning as much as they can about the products. And at the very least, they should purchase the product start-up package, the distributor kit, everything that's available to new distributors so they can learn the system quickly and thoroughly.

Worst

Choose the wrong opportunity.

This is an important decision that you're making. You should be very careful in selecting both a company and a sponsor. These are long-term relationships that you're putting in place. You need to give your initial decisions a great deal of thought, so that you can confidently stick with them.

Don't sign up with a sponsor via the Internet without having the slightest clue who that person is. Not only is it inefficient, but it's also the wrong way to choose someone, because you don't know if you'll have any chemistry between you.

Likewise, remember that just because someone gives a great presentation at the front of the room, that doesn't mean that they're going to be the right sponsor to help you. Be selective when you choose a company and sponsor. It will save everyone's time.

First

Focus on being duplicable.

The beauty of the business model behind network marketing is that it's designed to make success within the reach of ordinary, everyday people. So if you try to get too clever with your own unique ways of doing things, many people who would have been successful duplicating the tried-and-true methods would conclude that this business isn't for them. And you lose the potential participation of top producers.

In the 20 years I've been in this business, I've heard and considered hundreds of ideas to improve our reach. For example, I once thought it would be a good idea to buy a full-page ad in a major international newspaper. It would have been a great way to get the message out on a large-scale basis, and I could afford it. But then I realized that I would be modeling the wrong thing. My target market wouldn't have been able to duplicate that. And they would know it. So I changed my mind.

It's essential to use the business-building techniques that are available for everybody to use when they decide to join the business. That way you'll have more people who can see themselves in the business, and therefore will be more likely to enroll with you. And, in turn, when you encourage your team members to use business-building techniques that are duplicable by ordinary people, more people will enroll with *them*.

That's how your grow your organization.

Sonia Stringer

" Successful leaders carry a huge weight on their shoulders. They need people to talk to for emotional support.

Whether they find them in their own company or a mastermind group outside the company, they need someone to turn to when things get tough. It's really imperative. "

Best

Seek out the support you need.

I have found that successful people have a world-class support team around them. Sometimes they're lucky enough to be on the right team, with the right leader, in the right company. But there's almost always room for additional kinds of support.

There are three kinds of support that make a big difference. The first is strategic support. Find the tactics and strategies that someone in your upline (or a proven leader) is using. And then do your best to duplicate them. You can also get strategic support by being a member of a mastermind group. Support each other by sharing the best strategies. And then bring those strategies back to your team so you can all travel that learning curve quickly.

The second is emotional support. That's critical. When you become an entrepreneur, you're going to be facing a lot of challenges. And you need a lot of emotional support. You need encouragement. You need someone to be a cheerleader because there will be days when it's tough and you will want to give up. Consciously create an emotional support team you can count on at any time.

The third is support with the details. Even though this is a home-based business, you're running a million dollar business. So why try to do it all yourself? The leaders who develop the fastest are the ones who delegate. This allows them to focus on activities that make them money and the things they're truly brilliant at.

Worst

Measure success only by the results.

Too many people think they're only succeeding if they are seeing certain results in their business or paycheck. Obviously this isn't a hobby. You want to have results. But expand your vision of what winning looks like. Look at all the ways you're winning as you grow and develop the skills you'll need to succeed in the long run. How are you developing in your confidence and skill levels? Who are you meeting and how are you impacting people?

It's going to take time to get the financial results you want. But you can feel like you're winning from the very beginning if you acknowledge your growth and development every day.

Celebrate your growth and improvement as you go. It's a mindset that will help you stay encouraged and notice even the smallest of results. They may seem insignificant at the moment, but they really aren't.

First

Become an influencer.

If people are struggling, it's not because they don't have a great product or great business opportunity. Those things are usually a given now. But where the real struggle still is for some people is their ability to influence others to see the value of the business or the products.

But it's more than just salesmanship. Influence is about being authentic and heart-centered. It's about caring about people and believing you have something of value for them. And there some mechanics of influence that anyone can learn; some basic psychology, how to connect, how to create rapport, how to communicate in a way that expresses the value of what you have. So study influence and adapt its elements to your own personality. And be real throughout the entire process, no matter what.

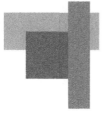

Jackie Ulmer

" So many people are blowing it because they're missing the authenticity component in building relationships online. For whatever reason, they forget the fact that there is a human being on the other end of the communication method they're engaged in – whether it's Facebook, instant messaging, texting, or email. **"**

Best

Develop real relationships online.

The way to go about creating authentic relationships online is to be who you would be offline. Take a legitimate interest in the people who you meet, and do so without a hidden agenda. Don't be in a hurry to hit the 5,000 friend mark. It's more about the quality of your relationships than the quantity.

Focus on meeting people you have something in common with. Start with people you already truly know. Expand from there. Who did you go to school with? How about your previous jobs? Groups? Clubs? Those are people in your warm market already. Now they're also in your online world. Expand and develop those relationships.

It's a tool like everything else. But people who go into online marketing first often do it out of fear. And eventually when they get prospects, they're going to have to answer the same questions and overcome the same objections that they would in their warm market.

They still need to know how to explain the opportunity and how to use the tools their company provides. If they don't already know how to do that, then the Internet isn't going to be an easier or better way for them.

Every single person who goes online looking for business also has a warm market. So by not going to your warm market, you're losing a big opportunity.

Worst
Spend money on paid advertising.

People who come to you through advertisements are still cold leads. They may not necessarily be any more interested in you than what they read in your little blurb in the ad. You still have to go through the process of warming them up and generating that trust that will make them receptive to hearing about your opportunity.

Paying for advertising isn't very duplicable either. You may have the money to spend on advertising, but the people you will be attracting probably won't. Paid advertisements are okay if you're selling a product, but not when you want to educate others about your business and have them duplicate what you're doing, and achieve success.

First
Use social media to expand locally.

Meetup is a great way to begin. It's keyword-oriented. So you can select groups that are based on your interests and mileage parameters. This is a great way to meet professionals who are looking for a change or who share your interests, like book clubs, fitness groups, etc.

Do a personal inventory of all your interests and topics that interface with your business. Then start looking online for groups of people who share those interests.

If I were to move to a new town today, I'd start with Meetup, and then LinkedIn, and Facebook. These will introduce you to all sorts of new groups to get in front of. You may decide that for some reason or another a specific group isn't for you. But you could also make just one contact in that group who could be "The One."

You'll have to sort through the people you meet this way. But you have to sort through people anyway.

Dana Wilde

" Network marketing is one of the few areas where someone who has no college education and relatively small means, can come in, make a big splash, and live the dream. If you want to learn and if you believe in yourself, the sky's the limit.

The industry feeds the adventurous spirit and the soul's need for freedom. I came into it after 10 years in Asia living out of a backpack. It was my next adventure, and it allowed me freedom, as well as creating abundance for myself and others. "

Best

Create a different list of *whys*.

You've already been told to make a list of *whys* around why success is important to you. I want you to make a different list. This is a list of all of the reasons why you will be successful ... your list of assets. What are your past successes? What skills do you bring to the table? What are your talents? What are your special experiences? Who are the people who will support you? What are your character traits that make you perfect for network marketing and network marketing perfect for you?

The only thing that makes us successful is the way we see ourselves in relationship to where we're going and what we bring to the table. You can spin any character trait you have for your success. Are you extroverted? Great! You make friends easily. You can talk to any stranger and make them happy to have met you. Are you introverted? Great! You're a good listener. You give other people the opportunity to shine in your presence. You give the leaders in your organization the chance to inspire others.

There is a part of the brain called the "reticular activating system," whose job is to find matches in your outside world to what you're thinking about. If you spend your time developing and studying your list of the reasons why you have what you need to be successful, your outside world is going to match that list seemingly effortlessly. You're training yourself to have positive expectations.

You're basically giving your brain an order list. You are telling your brain, "These are the things I want you to match up."

Worst

Focus on disappointments.

All of us are going to have experiences, goals, and projects that don't work out. Give them one second of your attention and then ignore them completely. Don't focus on anything that's going wrong in your business. Remember the reticular activating system? It will take that negative focus and match it with more negative experiences.

Focus only on your successes. You have everything it takes to be successful right now without fixing anything. The only thing you need to do is focus on your successes and trust in your bigger vision. When you have a disappointing experience, look at that list of assets you created, and keep on trucking.

First

Develop a mantra.

Create a short, catchy phrase that you can run in the back of your mind. Make it a positive message that you focus on throughout the day, and something you can consciously call up when you're facing a challenge to your confidence.

Popular mantras include, "Things always work out for me," "Abundance flows to me," "I'm on my way," "This is easy," "Things are unfolding perfectly."

The more general in nature, the better. If you get too specific (like "I see myself walking across the stage in my purple dress in April"), you'll have a hard time believing it. And the anxiety that arises will counteract the positivity, peace of mind, and confidence that you're developing with your mantra. Also, when you set specific goals that seem like ambitious stretch goals to your conscious mind, you might actually be limiting yourself. How do you know that you're not capable of even more, better and faster, if you just let your unconscious mind do the work for you?

Mark Yarnell

" Where else can you find something that's this much fun? You can work as much as you want. Or as little as you want. You don't have employees or overhead. There are no accounts receivable, no computer downtime. You get paid to talk to quality people. You mean I get paid to talk to nice people? I'm in. "

Best

Select a daily exposure number.

Professionals get paid; amateurs don't get paid. You are paid to recruit people to build a network and to retail products. So you must pick a certain number of hours every day when you're going to be professional and see how many people you're going to expose to your company.

Everyone who makes money goes through five stages: Expose, present, validate, enroll, and support. Exposure is the money step. This is a numbers game. The more people you talk to, the more presentations you're going to do. The more presentations you do, the more validations you're going to have, and then the more you enroll and support. The exposure step is the only step you have total control over. The people who expose the most to the largest number of people make the most money.

Pick the hours of the day when you will be doing one of two things: recruiting people into the business or retailing your product. Those are the only activities that you will be paid to do. Turn off all distractions that could tear you away from focusing on being anything but professional during that time.

Worst

Depend on technology too much.

We're a relationship marketing profession. And people are trying to figure out how to do it without building relationships. I don't think that's possible. The greatest strategic advantage is still face-to-face, or voice-to-voice, communication.

The great thing about technology is that you can spread information in a hurry. But if you use technology and leads to acquire people, the acquisitions are of no value to you because people who are addicted to technology are too distracted to do network marketing. Don't try to get people to change careers using technology. They're not going to get a single tweet or an email from you and give up their professions.

I'm not sending tweets or emails. I'm actually talking to other human beings and building relationships with them. My willingness to do that gives me a strategic advantage. Most people waste at least two hours a day on technological distractions. Why not turn that time into relationship-building, money-making activities? Wouldn't you rather use that time making $100,000 a month instead? Just turn off the technology.

Also don't use lead lists that are developed through technology. A lot of people go broke believing that all they have to do is get lead lists and work those. Lead lists don't work. I'm not saying that all lead lists are scams. But I never met anyone who bought leads and built a $25,000 a month check.

First

Build a data-specific list.

Everyone has 50,000 people in their warm market. Your warm market is not your friends and family. Your warm market is any group of people who will warm up to you when they find out you have something in common – you have an affinity of some kind. The first thing you do is get a data-specific list created based on your avocation, vocation, high school, town, whatever commonality will give you instant rapport with a stranger. These people are unique to you and will warm up the minute they find out your commonalities. And the more obscure and specific the list the better. That's why you'll never find yourself in a competitive situation.

It's instant warmth because you have an affinity; and you have an instant bond. And you're off to the races. You'll have more people that you can possibly talk to in your first two years.

Leslie Zann

" Our industry allows us to step into our greatness. You can be as outstanding as you choose to be—without limits. No limits on the amount of money you make ... no limits on the high-caliber person you can become. Whatever difference your business makes for you and others, its greatest gift may be your opportunity for personal development.

Where else can you be your own boss, create the lifestyle of your dreams, and become the best person you can be? Celebrate your opportunity! "

Best

Embrace personal development.

If any area of your life leaves you unsatisfied – from your relationships and health to your finances and career – commit to personal development and discover how to step into your greatness and design the life of your dreams.

Spend at least 15 to 30 minutes a day working on yourself ... not your job or your business. Include time to read or listen to positive information that reminds you how unlimited your possibilities truly are.

Have you ever wondered why so many lottery winners are broke within a few years of winning it big? I believe it's because their self-confidence, their self-worth, and their self-deserve never rose to the level of their new-found wealth.

Don't let this happen to you! Through the daily practice of personal development you can ensure that your self-confidence, self-worth, and self-deserve will rise to the level necessary to access the potential available to you with your business ... and lead you to your ultimate success.

Worst

Choose a slow pace.

People say they're excited when they jump in. But their actions don't always match their words. Many people just dabble or take a casual attitude, leaning in lightly, and taking it easy until it stops being fun.

The truth is, the pace you set in your first 90 days foreshadows your long-term success. The faster you go as you begin, the better the odds you will meet your goals and succeed at the level you desire.

So jump into your company's Fast Start program and pick up the pace in your first 30, 60, and 90 days. In fact, it's never too late to duplicate the activities of your company's Fast Start program and improve your pace. This gives you success stories that create interest in your business, which supports your sponsoring efforts.

It's more fun to go fast! The faster you start creating results, the better the odds that you will go the distance. The faster you achieve, the faster you'll believe in yourself and your business, and the more confident and coachable you'll become.

First

Be coachable.

I call it surrender—surrender to the system. The more coachable you are, the faster you'll surrender to the system.

Virtually every network marketing company has a proven business system in place. It's up to you to learn and master the system. Put your ego aside and be the best student you can because the system gives you tremendous advantages.

It doesn't matter who your sponsor is or whether you live in a big or small town. It doesn't matter if you've sold before, never sold before, or are starting out broke. When you rely on the system, everyone has the same opportunity to succeed and earn residual income.

Follow the system and you'll go fast. Try to reinvent the wheel or do it your way, and you'll go slow.

Do yourself a favor. Be coachable and go fast!

Tony & Sarah Zolecki

" **Sarah**: I love that moment when people discover that they can be financially successful just being themselves. People get to be fully alive for the very first time in their life. It's so inspiring and liberating.

Tony: For me, the reward of network marketing is seeing people get excited as they revive dreams they shelved so many years ago. They get so inspired with the hope that there's a solution for them, their families, and their loved ones. **"**

Best

S: Present to partners together.

When you're introducing the business to people, make sure that if they are in a relationship they bring their partner along. We even ask prospects if they're dating anyone. This way couples can make an educated decision together. When couples see it for the first time together, one isn't in the difficult position of having to explain an unfamiliar business concept to the other one later. When they see the opportunity together as a couple, they also have the benefit of your knowledgeable support and won't have to defend it to a resistant partner.

T: Communicate your commitment.

When you're telling your own partner about the new opportunity, make it clear that you're "all in." Your partner has to know that this isn't something that's just going to blow over in a couple of days, a couple of weeks, or even a couple of months. It's important that you say something like, "I still have a big dream of who I want to become and what I want to accomplish. This is something that I'm taking very seriously."

Worst

S: Don't involve your kids.

Your children may be too young to actively participate in helping you grow the business. But they're not too young to feel the effects of your intense focus. Help them see the bigger picture of what you're dreaming of for your family. Make sure you build in rewards to celebrate achieving short-term goals – the kinds of rewards that are meaningful to them. You're going to be teaching them so many great lessons – how to keep a dream alive, how to work hard for it, and how good it feels to celebrate when goals are met.

T: Force your family to participate.

If your partner doesn't want to actively participate with you, that's okay. That just means that you two have different interests in this one area of your lives.

Just bear in mind that your spouse might feel left out or worry that you're outgrowing the relationship. You have to remember to make time for your partner. Sarah and I have a specific date night every week. We go out to dinner and don't talk business. We make sure all our phones are off. We take the time to remind each other that we're still important to each other, no matter what else is going on in the business or world.

First

S: Get that first check ASAP.

In any situation, it's so important for a new person to start seeing tangible returns on their efforts. But it's even more essential when there's someone at home who isn't quite onboard with the idea of network marketing. When those checks start coming in, even if they're small in the beginning, it's proof that the business model works. All of a sudden the partner who wasn't supportive becomes network marketing's biggest advocate – sometimes even the star builder on your team!

T: Focus on short-term goals.

Think of your business in terms of 90-day micro-bursts. You go all out for 90 days, achieve those goals that you celebrate as a family, take a breather for a short time, and then do another micro-burst. You're going to be tired, and your family is going to be out of balance for those months you're in micro-burst mode. And that's okay. As long as your family knows that it's not a permanent condition, they are in a position to handle it better.

The very nature of starting any business is messy. So just be grateful with where you are in your life and business. No matter what it is – good, okay, not so good – be grateful. And be excited about this journey your entire family is on.

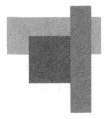

Our Contributors

Jordan Adler was not an overnight success. Eleven years and 12 companies after he first signed onto network marketing, his first distributor joined his team. Since then he has earned almost $20 million in network marketing. When he's not traveling the world growing his network marketing business, he divides his time between Las Vegas, NV, and the mountains of Arizona. In his free time, he flies helicopters and promotes his *Beach Money* books and seminars.

Margie Aliprandi, *Have It All* coach, is a 26-year network marketing veteran with a team of more than 250,000 in 29 countries. She's been ranked 61 among the top 500 network marketing earners worldwide, and is in the top 1% of network marketing producers worldwide. As a speaker/trainer for network marketing and general business audiences, she has coached and inspired hundreds of thousands of people. Her work is based on the strategies and time-tested principles behind her real-world success, and is the basis for her bestselling book, *How to Get Absolutely Anything You Want.*

Tom Alkazin, and his wife **Bethany**, are the top earners in their company and highly ranked in the Network Marketing Hall of Fame. With lifetime earnings over $22 million, they built up a team of 350,000 distributors and customers who have enrolled in their organization, with a strong presence in the United States, Asia, and Europe. Well over $125 million in sales flow through their organization as a result of their decision to start in the direct selling industry. They live in a gorgeous 6,000 sq. ft. home in Carlsbad, CA, near the Pacific Ocean. Their three children are also involved in the business.

Eric Allen is leading the charge in cultivating a more mainstream and well-respected image of the network marketing profession. He currently has a team of over 45,000 in 23 countries. As a former teacher and basketball coach, Eric and his wife **Casey** now live an amazingly abundant lifestyle and are able to spend all their time with their three sons and pursuing the causes they are passionate about. Eric believes that network marketing provides anyone who is coachable, teachable, and maintains a strong *why* a tremendous vehicle for complete life transformation.

Jen Audette was a dental hygienist when she discovered network marketing. Initially, she began her business to help defray mounting medical bills, and she discovered network marketing during a search on her computer for "home-based business." In her first two years, she earned six figures working part-time. Not only did she pay off the family medical bills, she was also able to save for her children's college education, and travel throughout the United States, Canada, Mexico, and the Caribbean.

Janine Avila is a highly respected international success coach, keynote speaker, mentor and success strategist. For over 25 years, she has been an icon in network marketing, both as a top performing field leader and as senior vice president of sales and marketing at the corporate level. Janine's team-building and time-management

techniques helped her lead the world in Tupperware promotions in the 1980s by consistently breaking records in
sales, recruiting, and rank advancements for her team.
Janine is currently the number one income earner in her
new company. And she enjoys her freedom to spend time
with her seven children and 18 grandchildren at her ranch
in the foothills of Yosemite, CA.

Kevin and **Pamela Barnum** met working as undercover police officers. Kevin went on to a become a canine
handler and Pamela a prosecuting attorney – not your
average entrepreneurs. Their passion and commitment
to integrity propelled their network marketing business
earning them numerous awards, including their company's Fastest Growing Business internationally. They've
grown their business to over $1 million in less than four
years – working fewer than 10 hours a week.

Kody Bateman is the founder and CEO of one of
the fastest growing companies in the United States. Kody
was born and raised in Salt Lake City, where he lives with
his wife **Jody** and his family. Since reading *How to Win
Friends and Influence People* at 16, he has wanted to be an influence for good in people's lives by helping them live positive and successful lives. He has been a featured speaker at
over 200 network marketing events and conducts personal
development seminars for audiences all over the United
States, Canada, and Australia.

Calvin Becerra became a million dollar income
earner his first year in network marketing and is now
ranked in the top class of his company after only six
years in the profession. He specializes in building teams

internationally. A graduate cum laude with a Bachelor's degree in criminology and pre-law, his network marketing income allows him to pursue real estate and mortgage banking, as well as spending quality time with his family and traveling the world.

Tina Beer is a top income earner and well-respected leader in network marketing. A former flight attendant who discovered network marketing from a catalog found in a seatback pocket of 13 years ago, she traded her shiny gold wings for residual income and time freedom. Tina's heart and purpose is to serve others. She teaches and trains thousands in her organization how to pursue their own dreams and desires. Tina's passion is to help others realize that it's truly possible to create and live a life by design, not by default.

Ty Bennett began his entrepreneurial career at age 21 when he started a business with his brother Scott, which grew to over $20 million in revenue while they were still in their 20s. He has spoken to more than a million people from 50 countries about leadership, influence, entrepreneurship, and storytelling. He is the author of *The Power of Influence* and *The Power of Storytelling*, as well as the video training programs, *Facts Tell, Stories Sell*.

BK Boreyko embraces the personal and corporate philosophy to make a positive difference in people's lives. Embracing the principle that long-term health is something people need to invest in today, BK leveraged his 20 plus years of experience in the wellness industry with his passion for creating unique ways to keep people healthy and founded his own Scottsdale, AZ, based network marketing company. An advocate of paying it forward, BK devotes much of his personal and corporate resources to giving back to the world through philanthropic projects.

Richard Bliss Brooke is a 35-year network marketing veteran, a former member of the board of directors of the Direct Selling Association, a senior member of the DSA Ethics Committee, and the owner of two network marketing companies. In 1977, Richard left his job chopping chickens to join network marketing. After four years, he was earning $40,000 a month with over 30,000 active partners. He earned his first $1 million before age 30. Richard is the author of *Mach II, The Art of Personal Vision and Self-Motivation, The Four Year Career*, as well as dozens of articles, audios, and videos.

Masa Cemazar is originally from Slovenia and spent 10 years doing medical research before a 17 year old girl introduced her to network marketing 8 years ago. She became one of the youngest Diamonds in her first company in less than 2 years and has been a top income earner with her current company for the past 5 years. She speaks 6 languages and lives in Brisbane Australia and works in her business together with her husband Miguel Montero.

Onyx Coale is a 47-year-old mother of three. As a single mom, she built a huge global organization of over 400,000 people. Onyx loves watching people become fully present in their MLM business. And she takes special pleasure in watching other woman build an income that allows them choices in their lives. Onyx lives in south Florida with her three beautiful girls. She has recently gotten engaged to the man of her dreams.

Dana Collins realized 18 years ago that having a successful career in corporate America meant placing her priorities on the back burner. The right network marketing opportunity came along, and Dana saw the possibility of building an incredible income without sacrificing her priorities. Within 10 years, Dana built a multimillion-dollar organization, consistently earning the highest awards from her company as a Top 10 Income Earner. She continues to inspire others in her organization, as well as the network marketing community over all, as a speaker, mentor, and coach. She lives in Savannah, GA, with her three children.

Chris Cucchiara's roots lie in world-class bodybuilding, but he brings that same world-class drive and inspiration to everything he does in life. Chris began his network marketing career in 1995 as a single dad. Because of his burning desire to succeed, he became one of the fastest growing distributors and income earners in his first company. Today, he is a nationally recognized leader having built large organizations and reaching the top pay plan in multiple companies. Through his mind-fit teaching philosophy, he has enjoyed seeing thousands of people reach entirely new levels of personal satisfaction, growth, and financial success.

Jane Deuber's vast experience in the direct selling profession includes a 13-year position as founder and CEO of her own party plan company, a six-year position as a co-founder of the Direct Selling Women's Alliance and over 26 years helping direct sellers advance to higher levels of leadership with their company. She was lead writer for two best-selling books, *Build It Big* and

More Build It Big. Her programs incorporate proven best practices with inner game strategies that empower you to transform both your business and life.

Ken Dunn began his professional life in investigative policing (narcotics, surveillance, fraud, interrogation, homicide) in Canada, where he spent time honing skills that would serve him throughout his business career, which included starting a mortgage origination company. Ken sold that business in 2005 to become a full-time network marketing professional. Over the next decade, Ken has helped to build business in three companies, which has resulted in hundreds of thousands of distributors. Today Ken is the co-owner of a successful network marketing business that operates in over 10 countries and yields millions in revenue annually.

Sandy Elsberg began her career as a first grade teacher in one of New York City's most notorious ghettos. In 1981, network marketing caught Sandy's attention. By applying her teaching skills, only fine-tuned for adult audiences, Sandy skyrocketed to the top of the earners charts, and has remained there for 30 years. She teaches the only accredited course on network marketing at the University of Illinois at Chicago, with Charles King, Tim Sales, and Mark Yarnell. She is a regular contributor to industry magazines and keynote speaker for high-level trade association and industry events.

Sean Escobar achieved six-figure income success at the age of 23, and million-dollar income earner status by 27 – a record for his company. Sean and his wife, **Crystal**, live in Utah with their three children, keeping

alive his dream to work from home, helping people overcome self-limiting attitudes and realize the full power of
their potential. He now owns three magnificent homes in
different parts of the country, enabling him to enjoy the
blessing of traveling with his family and working from
wherever his heart desires.

Tony and **Randi Escobar**, in addition to being
Sean's parents, have built an organization exceeding 1.2
million members. They are the only network-marketing
professionals to receive prestigious commendations from
Congress, as well as governors of 14 states. Tony and
Randi were also nominated for the *Guinness Book of World
Records* for building the largest organization and earning
them most money in the shortest period of time. They
were selected by Jack Canfield to represent the network
marketing profession in his runaway bestseller, *The Success Principles.*

Kimmy Everett discovered network marketing as a
single mom struggling to pay her rent. Although she loved
her job as a fundraiser for a popular school in Hawaii, she
didn't love her 60 hour-a-week schedule or the low pay.
Within 90 days of working her business part time, she
reached the top level of leadership in her company. Her
secret to success lay in building her business simply, quickly, and most importantly – coming from the heart with everyone she met. Kimmy's authentic approach to business
attracted people who previously "weren't that interested in
network marketing" into her team, and helped her create
one of the fastest growing organizations in the field.

Todd Falcone has over 20 years of full-time experience in network marketing and direct selling, and now

devotes all his time to teaching on the subject. He has devoted his entire professional life to achieving expertise and mastery, conducting thousands of conference calls, webinars, and live events in front of tens of thousands of people in every country throughout the world. He is president of Reach4Success, LLC, and is the author of numerous articles and training programs, including *Insider Secrets to Recruiting Professionals, How to Win in the Game of Prospectings, The Little Black Book of Scripts,* and *The Fearless Networker.*

Ann Feinstein, and her husband **David**, are Executive Diamond Directors serving on their company's worldwide Leadership Advisory Council. Named one of the Top 100 Direct Selling Mentors, Ann is a featured speaker and trainer at many international network marketing professional events. While actively participating and contributing to many of their company's charitable global projects, Ann and David were honored with the prestigious Global Ambassador, Inspiration of the Year, and Drivers of the Year awards, as well as inducted into their company's Hall of Fame.

Richard Fenton and **Andrea Waltz** are the authors of the book, *Go For No! Yes is the Destination, No is How You Get There.* They have made it their mission to liberate people from fears of failure and rejection, sharing an entirely new mindset about hearing the word *no.* The philosophies have been embraced by people in a wide variety of industries and businesses with rave reviews and amazing results. *Go for No!* has remained in the top 20 of books in the sales category on Amazon for the last three years.

Janine Finney and **Lory Muirhead** are mother and daughter, respectively. Lory quickly realized after graduating from college with a Bachelor's in marketing, communications and Spanish, that she didn't fit into the structure of a traditional career. She craved freedom and flexibility, and she wanted the opportunity to make an unlimited income based on her effectiveness. When she was introduced to network marketing, she immediately recognized that this would provide the lifestyle that she had envisioned. Janine's background included over 30 years in sales and business development in corporate America. After initially refusing to join Lory, she decided to jump in with both feet. Janine and Lory have built their own successful organizations side by side. They are also the co-authors of the book, *The Flip Flop CEO*, about the brilliance of being able to earn a CEO income in your flip flops.

Doug Firebaugh began network marketing in 1985, and spent the next 14 years helping to build and co-lead a home-business organization that spanned eight countries and produced hundred of millions in sales. He then formed PassionFire International, now Doug Firebaugh Training International, which trains home based professionals in every aspect of the profession, network marketing, social media, and team building mastery. Doug has also consulted with dozens of CEOs and presidents of home-based business companies. Providing training in over 30 countries, he believes in the philosophy that we are created by God to succeed, not survive, to live a life of victory and not a life of victimhood.

Tyler Ford, and his wife **Mimi**, have a passion for health and nutrition. Athletic enthusiasts, they enjoy

294 Aliprandi & Finney

the outdoors, riding and racing their road and mountain bikes, swimming, and competing in triathlons. Their mission is to enrich the quality of people's lives through better health and increased wealth. They believe that, "There are many things in life you get a second chance at, like relationships, finances, and careers. Your health is one thing that you do not get a second chance at. So why not take care of yourself?"

Randy Gage has trained more network marketing millionaires than anyone alive today. He helped introduce network marketing in developing countries and trained the top income earners in dozens of companies. He teaches from real-world experience, earning millions of dollars as a distributor and leading a team of over 200,000. He is also the author of nine bestselling books and dozens of audio and video resources on success that have been translated into more than 25 languages and sold millions of copies around the world. His *Duplication Nation* is the top-selling training album in network marketing; and *Escape the Rat Race* is the number one recruiting tool.

Puya Ghandian discovered the world of personal development at age 17. He instantly recognized the value of studying books, such as *Think and Grow Rich* by Napoleon Hill, and applying their principles. For example, he says, "I learned that going the extra mile makes a difference." He employed that truth while working as a receptionist at an advertising company. "I arrived earlier and stayed later than everyone else. I was never afraid of hard work, and they noticed." Within two years, at age 23, he became a vice president at the company. At first he was thrilled with the promotion, but before long Puya realized his life was all work and no play. He had become a slave to his job. When a trusted friend posted a comment on Facebook about a new business venture, Puya responded instantly. "I had learned it's important to hang out with people who have their stuff together, and this guy did." Today, Puya enjoys sharing personal-development lessons with others. "I'm not all about work," he says. "Like other people still in their 20s, I have lots of fun."

Kirk Gillespie, national sales director, sales and business coach, speaker and trainer, has led thousands in her organization to their personal successes. For over 30 years, she has followed her passion to empower women with greater confidence, sustainable income, and a values-based lifestyle by teaching them how to grow a business of their own around the things they love. Her mission is to encourage women to become the best they can be and live the life they dream of.

Amee Cleave became a top earner in her company after only five years in the profession. Well known for her high energy and expertise in relationship building, she is a stay-at-home mom, wife, inspirational speaker, personal coach, as well as continuing to be top income earner in her company. Amee is the founder of the *Get Your SPARKLE Back* series, inspiring women to find their purpose and turn their passion into profit.

Natalie Goddard was raised on a ranch as the seventh of eight children. Today as a holistic health coach she shares the message of health and hope around the world. As co-creator of the *Success Essentials System*, and co-author of *The Lead Guide*, she brings powerful tools to guide any authentic network marketer to success.

Debi Granite began her career in network marketing while she was struggling to start over after divorce and wondering what her next step in life would be. She previously owned a successful store, had a successful film and television career, owned her own film production company, and was part of several successful start-ups. Debi makes her home in Scottsdale, AZ, where she loves spending time outdoors, riding horses, skiing, golfing, power walking, and traveling. She also loves learning about quantum physics, the science of the mind, and exploring the wonders of our universe and healing arts.

Justin and **Keri Harrison**, along with their six young boys, are living their dream—all because they took a total leap of faith several years ago. Justin is passionate about helping others achieve health freedom, time freedom and financial freedom. In the 17 years he has worked in this profession, he has been a national trainer for a very large direct sales company, doubling the sales growth in a very short time. He has built several organizations over the years and currently supports a team of over 400K people and $25 million in monthly sales.

Ray Higdon helps network marketers recruit more representatives, get more leads, and become top earners in their network marketing business. He is the number one earner in his company, having earned more than $1 million, is a #1 Amazon best-selling author, and his blog receives over 2.5 million page views every month. He and his wife, **Jessica**, are passionate about helping others in this profession.

David Hsiung majored in electrical engineering. He became a human resource trainer, but eventually joined the family business, professional cosmetic sales. David and his wife, Tanya, moved to the United States in 2001, where they formed their own company, importing and exporting professional health equipment, to help the family business in Taiwan. In 2009, David joined network marketing to help a friend. He didn't plan on profiting in any way from the experience. David's attitude changed as he experienced the quality products and the integrity of the company. It seemed natural for David and Tanya to begin sharing. They decided to first focus on the success of others and as a result their own success followed.

Donna Imson is a successful networker, an accomplished trainer, public speaker, and thought leader in network marketing. As Executive Chairman of a leading direct selling company, she has enjoyed various accomplishments throughout the years, from being one of the 20 award recipients in the ANMP 2013 International Convention for her outstanding contributions to the profession of network marketing worldwide to being featured in the book, *The Greatest Networkers in the World*. With humble beginnings as a struggling single mother of three, Donna has become a role model for millions of entrepreneurial aspirants, especially women who are starting off in the industry.

Lisa Jimenez helps people break through fear and self-limiting beliefs to get into action and achieve their goals. As an international speaker and business coach, she teaches people how to retrain the brain and create the mindset they need to build a successful business and life. Her own success in direct sales came from setting one specific goal: Create financial freedom for five people.

That single focus helped her become a top income earner. Lisa's bestselling books *Conquer Fear!* and *Don't Mess With the Princess!* have sold over 250,000 copies and are published in seven languages. Her third book, *Radical Transformation!* will be released in 2014.

Donna Johnson has been a top income earner in network marketing for over 30 years. She continues to lead a vibrant business and is passionate about teaching and modeling sustainable, ethical business practices. Donna sits on the editorial board of the prestigious professional magazine, *Networking Times*, is the co-author of the book, *MLM CPR: Restart the Heart*, and wrote *Making a Living By Making a Difference*. The mother of five children and grandmother of three, she divides her time among her homes in Arizona, Wisconsin, and Sweden.

Art Jonak has one of the "feel good" stories that keep the dream alive for many. Twenty years ago he had to count on food stamps to buy baby food for his newborn daughter. In his quest to get out of debt, he worked two jobs and delivered pizzas at night. His relationships were horrible. Every aspect of his life was spiraling downward. So he joined network marketing. Today Art has travelled to 78 countries and has built an organization with distributors in 23 of those countries. He continues to help others reach significant leadership positions and income levels in the business.

Michelle A. Jones is at the top .01% of her company, which does $4.2 billion in sales and has 2.7 million distributors globally. Michelle started in corporate America making a six-figure income but realized that she was time poor. In 2004, she made the shift to direct sales due to the time freedom and financial freedom it allows. Through consistent, focused work the last three years, Michelle earned three free cars, has been on 19 earned trips, and has earned a $30,000 bonus for sales growth in a single month. In her free time, she loves to play golf, travel the world, and help others see the vision of this life-changing profession.

Kimber King has spent the last decade helping hundreds of people achieve success both financially and physically. Because of her passion to help others reach their own personal goals of health and wealth, Kimber has created a seven-figure income working part-time from her home, all while enjoying a balanced, rewarding, family, and charity-focused lifestyle, without sacrificing her values or priorities. Kimber is dedicated to serving God, her husband, and their three sons. She says, "My passion is to watch others succeed beyond what they thought was possible for their life! Most people just need someone to believe in them and show them simple steps to achieving the dreams they have in their hearts!"

Becca Levie is one of the top earners of her company, inspirational speaker and moving author. Her journey has taken her from being an abandoned child to being a leader where her profound insights, love for life, and its many opportunities are changing lives everywhere.

Tracy Monteforte is co-founder of WTPowers. com, an automated prospecting and training system that has helped thousands of network marketers world-wide build their businesses faster, bigger, and easier since 2001. A former junior high school teacher, and certified NLP

Master Results Coach, Tracy has taught thousands of network marketers the mindset, skill set, and tool set essential for successful telephone prospecting. Her mission is to teach network marketers how to finally overcome their internal obstacles and truly work 100% from home, leveraging the power of the Internet and the telephone.

Romi Neustadt was a lawyer and award-winning public relations executive when she began her business. She had no idea that it would quickly become her full-time profession with the flexibility she needed to make her children her top priority. In less than three years, she became one of her company's first Million Dollar Circle Achievers. She has received numerous awards from her company, including top recruiter, advisory board member, and hall of fame inductee. Romi's favorite part of this business is helping others design the lives they really want.

Jeff Olson, the author of the book *The Slight Edge*, has spent the last 30 years helping hundreds of thousands of individuals achieve better levels of financial freedom and personal excellence. Born and raised in Albuquerque, NM, his resume includes being one of the youngest airport managers in the country, the sales manager for intelligence systems, the CEO of Sun Aire of America, a company devoted to all aspects of solar energy and founder of The People's Network, one of the largest personal development training companies in the United States. In 2012 Jeff launched his own marketing company that grew from zero to $100 million in one year, becoming the first company in its industry to do so.

Ken Porter has been in network marketing for over 30 years, since he was 23 years old. Ken and his wife

Carol have since made over $30 million with their distributorship. They have over 3 million distributors and customers who have enrolled in their organization, with a strong presence in the United States and 20 countries throughout Asia and Europe.

Jules Price grew up outside of Washington, DC. After receiving a Bachelor's in psychology and music, she moved to New York City to pursue her passion of singing. She still performs all over the world with the New York City Ballet as one of their principal singers. In 2006, Jules relocated to Sarasota, FL, where she was introduced to her current network marketing company. With no previous background in the profession, Jules instantly saw the value of the product and the exciting opportunity it presented. She is now a corporate trainer, top income earner, and the author of the book, *Secrets from the SOC Drawer*. Jules is passionate about helping others to listen to life and achieve all the success they desire.

Paula Pritchard was teaching at Kent State University when she was introduced to her first networking experience. The company was Amway, where she would become the first single woman in the United States to reach the coveted Diamond Level. Since her time at Amway, she has achieved major success with five other network marketing companies. She spearheaded the expansion of three of those companies into Europe, building organizations of 200,000 people, producing hundreds of millions of dollars in business in over 15 countries. Today Paula is a master distributor and multi-million dollar earner with a successful company. She is also an author, public speaker, trainer and has consulted with both established and new network marketing companies in both the United States and Europe.

Bob Quintana has been a successful entrepreneur since 1989, and an accomplished management consultant, trainer and executive coach since 1992. In 2006, after realizing that his consulting company was always going to require his actively "chasing the next deal" (and the one after that) Bob and his wife Pennie shut down his very profitable consulting business and made a commitment to network marketing as his primary focus. Currently, Bob has reached the senior rank of Platinum Ambassador. Thanks to his rapidly expanding team, he has over 8,500 associates and well over 100,000 customers in his organization. He has served as chairman of his company's Associate Leadership Council – an advisory/field liaison organization to the corporation.

Jeremy Reynolds was a self-made millionaire by the time he reached his 32nd birthday. Before entering the network marketing profession as a distributor, he had started his own nutritional powder manufacturing company, with the slogan, "Be Ethical, Be Responsive, Be Profitable." Within five years, he built his company into a $30 million niche producer, which would serve the network marketing company he would ultimately join as a distributor. He may have owned his own company but he didn't own his own life. He recognized that network marketing professionals were making as much – or more – money that he was. But they also had time freedom. Today he is the founding distributor, ambassador, and multi-millionaire member of the company that was once his client.

Matthew Riddell is among the first of a new generation of Diamonds in his company. Working alongside a team of brilliant business leaders across Australia, where he lives, and the world, he teaches everyday people to build true information-age lifestyle businesses. He joined network marketing in September 2007 after seeing the potential for residual income and leadership opportunities that just didn't exist in the traditional paths. Lucky enough to work with industry giants on a daily basis, Matthew remains an active business leader showing people how they, too, can escape the rat race and live their dreams.

Sarah Robbins is a kindergarten teacher turned seven-figure annual residual income earner in network marketing, and is considered one of the world's leading network marketing consultants. Now in the top 1% income bracket of all women in America, she began part time with no business experience and had achieved a six-figure income by age 29. As a speaker, she contributes unique insights on success, prosperity, leadership, and network marketing topics. She is fulfilling her lifelong dream of helping others.

Teresa Romain is a dynamic and transformational speaker, trainer, and coach. Her gift is her ability to look at things differently and in a way that creates openings for people to break through the scarcity patterns that limit their ability to grow and thrive – personally and professionally. She is masterful in her ability to teach and support people to build a simple, practical, and sustainable foundation for living that allows them to prosper – financially, emotionally, and spiritually.

Hilde and **Orjan Saele** are the cofounders of a
network marketing company. Hilde was first inspired by
reading her grandfather's copy of *Think and Grow Rich*,
and joined the network marketing profession at age 20,
during her second year of law school. Over time she
learned the skills, figured out the balance between going
aggressively after a goal and having a soft heart... and
meeting to meeting, person to person, leader by leader
she built a successful network marketing business and
became a multimillionaire. Orjan earned over $10 mil-
lion in network marketing before reaching age 30. Orjan
built an organization that sponsored 5% of the entire
country of Norway (in the age group 20-60 years). From
there his team expanded to Sweden, Denmark, and Fin-
land with similar results.

Tim Sales was concluding an 11-year tour with the
U.S. Navy Underwater Bomb Squad Team when he answered an ad in *The Washington Post* that led him to his
first and only network marketing company. Five years later his network marketing income rose to over $150,000 a
month, with over 56,000 people in his organization, and
2,400 new distributors entering from 20 countries monthly. Tim is one of the most sought after advisors, speakers,
trainers in the industry. The foremost expert on how to
explain the differences among a pyramid scheme, Ponzi
scheme, and a legitimate MLM business, his *Brilliant
Compensation* program has educated over 1 million people
around the world about network marketing.

Tom "Big Al" Schreiter, a 40+ year veteran of network marketing, is one of the most successful people in
the history of network marketing. Most people who join

network marketing have a goal, are positive, but don't know what to say or do to make that goal come true. Tom shows them the exact words and actions to make their business work through his *Big Al Report*. Probably half of the top leaders in companies around the world today were weaned on Tom's "Big Al" book series and his "Live in London" tapes. Tom's a living legend in the business, having built the largest, most active database in network marketing history, assembling distributor organization of more than 100,000 people in just over two years, and founding two network marketing companies.

Jerry Scribner passed on going to college to join the sheetrock business owned by his father, who taught him a very strong work ethic at an early age. His first venture into sales was in 1984 when he answered a newspaper ad for selling insurance, got licensed but experienced little success. After other false starts in other jobs, in March 2007 Jerry watched a 15-minute video regarding a "business idea." He signed on with the goal of making $300-$400 a month to help get his two daughters through college. By 2011 he became the 9th top earner of his company.

Bill Silvester began his entrepreneurial life at age 34 when he opened a scuba diving business in Byron Bay, in Australia's northern New South Wales. After teaching thousands of people to scuba dive and building a business that generated over $700,000 a year, Bill and his wife, Sharon, sold their business, starting network marketing in 1989. In just over nine years, the couple achieved a senior rank and a consistently high-income level.

Sean Smith is father and husband first, speaker/ coach/seminar leader second. At the age of 13, he was almost killed by his next-door neighbor, which taught him that none of us, no matter what our circumstances, is promised our next breath. He vowed to himself to live a life of greatness, never settling for mediocrity. However, despite that promise, he still struggled for the next 20 years, until he learned the power of the unconscious mind. Sean is now a Certified Master Results Coach, and has mentored thousands of direct sales business owners to eliminate their fears, stop sabotaging themselves, create explosive success, and live their lives with passion, purpose, and presence.

Roman Sobolevsky started in network marketing 20 years ago out of despair. Political and economic upheavals in the Soviet Union had resulted in full loss of his property, his home, and any means to provide for his family. While he received the idea of network marketing with the typical reactions of skepticism and disbelief, his reading of the classic network marketing books quickly changed his mind. He applied their advice, and his organization grew very quickly. Roman adapted the methods and recommendations of American network marketers to the conditions and business philosophy in the post-Soviet market. And he was the first to create a well-structured, logical system of training, development, and motivation of distributors, leading thousands to prosperity. Today his organization is the largest in the Commonwealth of Independent States (which is a regional organization made up of countries that were once part of the Soviet Union).

Sonia Stringer is a speaker, author, business coach, and founder of Savvy Network Marketing Women – an online community that helps more than 50,000 women around the world bring big money and a bigger difference through their network marketing/direct sales business. For 17 years, Sonia has helped women at all levels (total newbies to seven-figure earners) to learn simple skills that make an immediate difference in their sales, team growth, and recruiting success – and to set up their businesses so they have more free time with their families and for other priorities.

Jackie Ulmer is a network marketing team leader, trainer, and author. She started in January, 1994, as a skeptic, and quickly fell in love with the advantages it offers. Six years later, she discovered the Internet. Today, she's built an international business and income using online methods to build her business while managing a family and a life. Blogging and social media are the platforms she uses and mentors on.

Dana Wilde has been named one of the top 50 most powerful and most influential people in direct selling and network marketing by *Direct Selling Live*. She is the trusted authority in creating positive mindset and fast business growth for entrepreneurs, sales professionals, and corporate leaders. She knows how to stimulate brain power for personal and professional achievement in individuals and teams everywhere. The creator of the revolutionary program, *Train Your Brain*, she has developed 20 "Mindware Experiments" used by top income producers from a variety of industries to rapidly increase their business growth.

Mark Yarnell is the author of 12 books, including the long-standing international bestseller, *Your First Year in Network Marketing* and the most recent releases *The Lotus Code* and *How to Become Filthy, Stinking Rich Through Network Marketing*. As a network marketing leader, Mark has built an organization of 300,000 people in 21 countries. He has educated thousands of entrepreneurs through his books, webinars, presentations, and private coaching.

Leslie Zann leads the industry at showing people how to recognize and unleash their true passion and limitless potential and overcome their potential-stopping, limiting beliefs. She built her own successful direct selling business ($1.2 million in sales), and has eight years' corporate experience with three distinct business models: Direct selling, network marketing, and party plan. With her innovative virtual course, *5 Keys to Outrageous Achievement*, and the CD program, *Outrageous Achievement*, Leslie is expanding her reputation as a go-to industry leader in personal development. As a raved-about speaker, trainer, and personal coach, Leslie challenges her clients to "be willing to see things differently." And in doing so, she has inspired tens of thousands to attain outrageous achievement in sales, sponsoring, and leadership development.

Sarah and **Tony Zolecki** are top leaders in their company with over 15 years' experience building their own network marketing businesses separately before meeting, falling in love, and marrying. Over the last seven years they've worked together as a couple to grow one of the largest teams in their company. Along the way, Tony and Sarah have picked up numerous awards and accolades, including "Leader of the Year" from among thousands of distributors. Their team has grown into a dozen different countries, providing them with the opportunity to travel extensively and inspire thousands of people around the world to dream bigger and create financial freedom.

About the Authors

Margie Aliprandi is living proof that it pays to stay, and it pays to persist. Now celebrating her 26th year with the same company where her journey began, she's a multi-millionaire network marketing icon with an unyielding passion for helping others be, do, and have all that life has to offer.

The idea of helping people grow themselves into greatness took root when she was a nine-year-old listening to a reel-to-reel recording of Russell Conwell's *Acres of Diamonds*. It was her first exposure to the concepts of personal development. Combined with the influence of her parents, these concepts ignited fires within.

Fast forward to Margie the teenager. Now she was delivering motivational speeches on self-esteem, setting high standards, pursuing big goals, and how to be truly happy. She didn't know it then, but the network marketing profession would become the logical outlet for her naturally emerging purpose.

Fast forward to Margie the junior high school music teacher and the 1989 series of events that would hint at the first gossamer outlines of her destiny. She fell in love with a fledgling network marketing company that offered a product so exciting that she knew she could talk about it passionately to anyone, anytime, anywhere. She'd need to start her own business despite the three strikes against her: Single mom with three little kids, no business experience, and no startup capital. And she wanted to give her children a better life. They were her *why*. So she decided to do "whatever it takes."

"Whatever it takes" meant a lot of things. Like taking off for distant business presentations in her Subaru wagon because she couldn't afford airfare; sleeping in her car because she couldn't afford hotels; dressing in gas station restrooms, and bouncing into meetings which at times consisted of a handful, or one, or even none of the expected audience. But look what happened anyway:

During her first year, more money in a month than she would have made in a year of teaching. Within three years, her first million dollars. Five years after that, a team of over 500,000 throughout Eurasia. Her team today remains among the largest in the world, spanning 29 countries, and teeming with millionaires. She's been ranked Number 61 among the top 500 earners, and listed in the upper 1% of producers, in network marketing worldwide. And through it all she's rebuilt her business three times over from scratch.

While continuing to support her team she's also expanding her ability to assist all aspiring entrepreneurs and elevate the profession as a whole through keynote speeches, training, and writing. The nine-year-old who couldn't get enough Russell Conwell grew up to specialize in transformational personal development as the essential step of the network marketing journey.

Today, Margie is the mother of four grown children, Shaun, Nicole, Todd, and Ashley. She divides her time in

San Diego, Salt Lake City, and Durango where her fiancé Ray Zwisler resides. Her most recent book is the bestselling book, *How to Get Absolutely Anything You Want*, which is available on Amazon.com.

Martha I. Finney is a Santa Fe-based business journalist and author of 19 books on leadership, entrepreneurialism, and career management. This has been her favorite book so far!

The daughter of an undercover CIA case officer, she was born in Munich during the height of the Cold War and moved once a year until she was 13 – to many of the Cold War hot spots as it unfolded, including Mexico City, Berlin, Miami, Madrid. That way of life left her with two characteristics that would mark her life forever – the yearning for travel and adventure, and the passion for striking up conversations with strangers. She could have joined the CIA herself (she even turned down an offer to run a safe house in New York City right out of college). But she chose to be a journalist instead.

Watching her father passionately dedicate himself to his own profession taught her that it was essential to have a mission in work that was all encompassing and that meant something larger than just a regular paycheck. So she dedicated her journalism career to telling the stories of how ordinary people achieve their full potential by doing the work they love, that brings them meaning, and that makes them happy.

Her own original research into joy in the American workplace has been reported in *The New York Times*, *The Washington Post*, *The Miami Herald*, *The San Francisco Chronicle*, *The Wall Street Journal*, *Time*, CNN and NPR's Morning Edition.

Acknowledgments

Margie and Martha would first like to thank our mutual friend, author Libby Gill, for bringing us together. It was one of those introductions that made the universe shift a little bit, and we owe it all to her.

We would also like to thank Allison Hays for her wisdom in seeing the "Best Worst First" concept as a stand-alone book.

Margie Aliprandi:

Thank you, Martha Finney. You merged my network marketing experience with your brilliant "Best Worst First" concept, your gifted writing, and your remarkable interviewing skills. We brought this book to life as yet another step along the pathway of helping business builders live the dream. Working with you has been a joy beyond description as we explored the worlds of 75 giants in network marketing.

Thank you, every one of those 75 giants, for your enthusiastic cooperation and superb contributions. The knowledge, wisdom, and heart you have so generously given have made this book a major, lasting asset for network marketers everywhere.

Thank you, my friends and mentors profession-wide, and thank you my dear team. You've probably taught me more than I've taught you. Your support has much to do with who I have become and with my contributions to this book.

Thank you, my parents – Mom, and Howard (my second father), and my dear Daddy Neil. You raised me to think expansively. This made it possible for me to identify with the network marketing business model when it came my way, and to remain emotionally resilient through the early lean times. Too many are not so fortunate. Too many are surrounded by naysayers.

Thank you, my now-grown children, Shaun, Nicole, Todd and Ashley – you were the *why* who got me started in this profession. Then you became the reason I did one of the most important things of all. I persisted, and I stayed.

Finally, thank you, Ray, my fiancé and soul mate, for your wonderful encouragement and support throughout the development of this book.

Martha Finney:

I mainly have Margie to thank for this fantastic opportunity to interview so many of her extraordinary, loyal friends for this book. These are relationships that have been built over the span of 26 years, and they clearly show what happens when you commit your life to helping others feel authentically wonderful about themselves. Margie's open-hearted affection and positivity lifted my spirits every time we connected to collaborate and interview these precious friends and colleagues of hers who trusted her unquestioningly. Watching her in action, I learned a lot more than simply what it takes to be world-class in network marketing.

I would also like to thank the talented Aidan Kallas, our designer and honchita extraordinaire. She took our shared vision for this book and turned it into this lively, happy look that you hold in your hands today. And then she took over the production piece, helping us hit all our deadlines – even while she was in the middle of a cross-country move and major life change. If you have a book of your own up your sleeve and you want it to look fabulous, let me know, and I'll put the two of you together.

Finally, a hat tip to both Ashley Roberts and Ginger Wilmot who kept our little book ball consistently moving forward. I seriously doubt that Margie and I would have been able to pull this off without your help!

Let's do this again sometime!

How to use this book to...

Build Your Team
&
Grow Your Check

For additional resources, news, events, information on discount pricing for bulk orders, visit:

www.bestworstfirst.com

P.S.: If you loved this book, please post a review on Amazon.com.

Share the love!